formatio

TRADITION. EXPERIENCE.
TRANSFORMATION.

Formatio books from InterVarsity Press follow the rich tradition of the church in the journey of spiritual formation. These books are not merely about being informed, but about being transformed by Christ and conformed to his image. Formatio stands in InterVarsity Press's evangelical publishing tradition by integrating God's Word with spiritual practice and by prompting readers to move from inward change to outward witness. InterVarsity Press uses the chambered nautilus for Formatio, a symbol of spiritual formation because of its continual spiral journey outward as it moves from its center. We believe that each of us is made with a deep desire to be in God's presence. Formatio books help us to fulfill our deepest desires and to become our true selves in light of God's grace.

Other books by Albert Haase, O.F.M.

Enkindled: Holy Spirit, Holy Gifts
  Coauthored with Bridget Haase, O.S.U.
  (St. Anthony Messenger Press, 2001)

Instruments of Christ:
Reflections on the Peace Prayer of St. Francis of Assisi
  (St. Anthony Messenger Press, 2004)

Coming Home to Your True Self:
Leaving the Emptiness of False Attractions
  (IVP Books, 2008)

Living the Lord's Prayer: The Way of the Disciple
  (IVP Books, 2009)

This Sacred Moment

BECOMING HOLY RIGHT

WHERE YOU ARE

⌒

ALBERT HAASE, O.F.M.

To Marelene
Stop. Look. Listen.
Respond—and come
one step closer to
holiness. Peace
[signature]

≋
IVP Books

An imprint of InterVarsity Press
Downers Grove, Illinois

InterVarsity Press
P.O. Box 1400, Downers Grove, IL 60515-1426
World Wide Web: www.ivpress.com
E-mail: email@ivpress.com

InterVarsity Press® is the book-publishing division of InterVarsity Christian Fellowship/USA®, a movement of students and faculty active on campus at hundreds of universities, colleges and schools of nursing in the United States of America, and a member movement of the International Fellowship of Evangelical Students. For information about local and regional activities, write Public Relations Dept., InterVarsity Christian Fellowship/USA, 6400 Schroeder Rd., P.O. Box 7895, Madison, WI 53707-7895, or visit the IVCF website at <www.intervarsity.org>.

Design: Cindy Kiple
Images: Ikon Images/Jason Jaroslav Cook/Getty Images

ISBN 978-0-8308-3543-0

Printed in the United States of America ∞

Library of Congress Cataloging-in-Publication Data

Haase, Albert, 1955-
  This sacred moment: becoming holy right where you are/Albert
Haase.
    p. cm.
  ISBN 9978-0-8308-3543-0 (pbk.: alk. paper)
  1. Holiness—christianity. 2. Christian life—Catholic authors. I.
Title.
  BT767.H23 2010
  248.4—dc22

2010024967

| P | 18 | 17 | 16 | 15 | 14 | 13 | 12 | 11 | 10 | 9 | 8 | 7 | 6 | 5 | 4 | 3 | 2 | 1 |
| Y | 25 | 24 | 23 | 22 | 21 | 20 | 19 | 18 | 17 | 16 | 15 | 14 | 13 | 12 | 11 | 10 |

"It is fulfilling the duty of the present moment, no matter in what guise it presents itself, which does most to make one holy."

CONTENTS

1

KNOWING HOLINESS
WHEN WE SEE IT

*J*osh, Brian and I had agreed to meet in a local coffee shop around 10:00 a.m. Brian and I chatted as we waited for Josh.

"Being a missionary in Alaska was both challenging and rewarding." Brian was summing up his three years among the Athabascan Indians. "The winter temperatures and the seasonal changing of daylight were a difficult adjustment. But I gradually got accustomed to both. The welcome and hospitality of the Indians were humbling. The members of this tribe are truly wonderful people; in so many ways, just like us, and in so many ways, very different from us."

"So what are your ministerial plans for the future?" I asked.

"Well, after a six-month sabbatical, I plan to go down to the missions in Brazil for five years. And after that, maybe I will dedicate five years to the missions in Russia," he replied.

I was so impressed with Brian's missionary spirit. I couldn't help but notice how he had the next decade of his life planned out. And I was amazed at how this Franciscan friar was truly becoming a missionary to the world. *He's really a holy man,* I thought.

We continued talking for forty-five minutes. Just as I was wondering whether to be irked or concerned about Josh's tardiness, Josh walked through the door of the coffee shop.

"I'm so sorry for being late!" he announced. "I would have made it on time but as I was driving over here, I noticed an elderly woman pulled over on the side of the road. She had a flat tire and clearly didn't know what to do. So I stopped and changed her tire."

Brian leaned over the table and said to Josh, "Your compassion and charity always challenge me."

I found it ironic that the "missionary to the world" whom I considered to be a saint was complimenting someone who had simply responded to an ordinary need. And then it hit me like a ton of bricks: maybe Josh's way was a better example of holiness.

What does it really mean to be a holy person? Do people like Brian exemplify it—those who have long-term plans for themselves that include missionary activity on different continents? Is it displayed in the person who says a lot of prayers and performs acts of penance? Or does it mean being a contemporary Elizabeth Fry, the nineteenth-century woman who founded schools, helped the Gypsies, took care of the homeless and earned the name "the angel of the prisoners" because of her ministry to those in jail? Is it demonstrated by someone like Dietrich Bonhoeffer, who successfully emigrated to New York but whose commitment to Christ challenged him to return to his native Germany and plot the downfall of the Nazi regime? Or does it mean renouncing power and possessions and living a life of heroic charity and compassion in the tradition of Mother Teresa of Calcutta?

The *Concise Oxford American Dictionary* defines the adjective *holy* as "(of a person) devoted to the service of God: *saints and holy men*" and "morally and spiritually excellent." However, in this day and age when we are so aware of the way different cultures, education and upbringing shape each human being uniquely, one person's act of godly devotion can be interpreted by another as an act of terrorism.

I thumb through the Gospels for an answer, since Christian holiness clearly has something to do with the imitation of Christ. But I find myself in a quandary since I'm not sure exactly what I am supposed to imitate and how far I should go. Am I supposed to go barefoot, become an itinerant preacher and gather disciples around myself? That seems naive and foolish—and maybe a bit egotistical.

Certainly Jesus' command to love God and neighbor cannot be overlooked. But how do I obey that command in a practical way on a daily basis? Am I supposed to have the same emotional feelings for a God I cannot see that I have for my closest friend? Even on my best of days, that doesn't seem possible. And how do I love the next-door neighbor whose name and personal history I don't even know?

The Sermon on the Mount (Matthew 5–7), daunting as it is, offers a lot of food for thought and action. I like to think of it as a compact handbook for holiness. It starts with the Beatitudes which clearly attack the agenda of the ego, focused as it is on self-concern, self-image, self-gratification and self-preservation. Much to the chagrin of the ego, Jesus calls "blessed" those who are not enslaved by the fantasies of consumerism but are poor in spirit and are willing to experience the painful emotions of grief and mourning. Jesus affirms those who renounce the lust for power and are meek. He encourages those who are willing to take a stand for justice and peace, who choose mercy over revenge and who are uncompromising in their lives as Christian disciples. Reflecting upon the Beatitudes certainly makes me realize that holiness has something to do with moving beyond the ego with its narcissistic concerns and hedonistic interests—a real "death to self."

The rest of the Sermon on the Mount offers some practical examples of Christian holiness. It reminds me that I cannot live a duplicitous life. I have to make a choice between the false attractions of the world—"treasures on earth"—and the eternal values of the gospel lifestyle—"treasures in heaven" (Matthew 6:19-21). Choosing heavenly treasures means putting all my concerns in the hands of God and trusting that God will care for my basic needs; a life of worry and anxiety betrays an obsession with trinkets and worldly pipe-dreams. The Sermon on the Mount challenges me to be nonjudgmental and to treat others as I myself would want to be treated. It also challenges me with the reminder that, when all is said and done, authentic disciples vote with their feet and not mere words.

Continuing through the New Testament, I come upon Paul's distinction between life according to the flesh and life according to the Spirit (Galatians 5:16-26). Clearly his understanding of life according to the flesh is a life consumed with, controlled by and centered upon the agenda of the ego. Giving full rein to the ego leads to a life of cheap, recreational sex; of outrageous demands and potential slavery to addictions; of putting exaggerated emotional investment in possessions; and of looking at other people through the eyes of a cutthroat competitor that depersonalizes them into potential threats or rivals. On the other hand, once a person moves beyond the puny yet well-fortified boundaries of the ego, their life blossoms with love, joy, peace, patience, kindness, generosity, faithfulness, gentleness and self-control. Life according to the Spirit is clearly a life of holiness.

And so, though it may be challenging to define Christian

holiness, we certainly know its fruits when we see them. We do, in fact, see the fruits reflected in the saintly lives of people, both past and present. The lives of Josh, Brian, Elizabeth Fry, Dietrich Bonhoeffer and Mother Teresa of Calcutta, for example, give witness to the enduring values of the Sermon on the Mount. They give evidence of the virtues which are characteristic of the Spirit of God; they strike us as "devoted to the service of God" and as being "morally and spiritually excellent." And what is the common thread of grace that is woven through these different lives from different historical periods and different Christian denominations? A selflessness that forms the heart of holiness.

REFLECTION QUESTIONS

You'll find a set of questions at the end of each chapter. These questions can be used for personal meditation, spiritual direction sessions or small group discussion.

1. Who comes to mind when you hear the word *saint?* Why? What qualities do these people possess?

2. Which Scripture passages illumine the path of holiness for you?

3. Is Christian holiness exhibited in a single act or in a lifetime of activity? Explain.

2

SELFLESSNESS AS THE HEART
OF HOLINESS

*T*hink again about my friend Josh who changed a flat tire for an elderly woman he didn't even know. I think his action says something quite important about holiness. Like countless others before him whom we consider to be holy, Josh selflessly responded to the need of the present moment. That reminds us that holiness is a lot simpler, less dramatic and, consequently, more challenging than most of us think.

By his own admission, Josh would have arrived at the coffee shop on time had it not been for his spontaneous response to a stranger's flat tire. Seeing her need, without even thinking about it, he pulled over and offered her a helping hand. I believe this is exactly what holiness is all about: it is *a selfless openness and response to God's call in this sacred moment.* And that call of God comes in the need that presently goes unmet or in the duty that is required in the present moment.

Holiness, then, is the lifelong journey out of slavery to the ego and its consuming preoccupation with self-concern self-image, self-gratification and self-preservation. It begins when we move out of the house of mirrors that most of us choose to live in and take up residence in a house of glass where we are constantly looking beyond ourselves, our concerns, our interests and our worries. It begins with selflessness.

A PERFECT EXAMPLE

Paul tells us that Jesus provides the perfect example of self-lessness. In the letter to the Philippians, he encouraged the church, "Let each of you look not to your own interests, but to the interests of others. Let the same mind be in you that was in Christ Jesus" (Philippians 2:4-5). The apostle explained this mindset by saying that Jesus did not exploit his equality with God and use it to his own personal advantage or for his own personal gain. Rather, he "emptied himself, taking the form of a slave" (Philippians 2:7).

To the Corinthians, Paul wrote, "For you know the generous act of our Lord Jesus Christ, that though he was rich, yet for your sakes he became poor, so that by his poverty you might become rich" (2 Corinthians 8:9). This becoming poor to enrich the lives of others, or "self-emptying," formed the very backbone of Jesus' ministry. We see it in the incarnation, in Jesus' friendship with sinners and the marginalized, in his total dedication and obedience to the will of his Abba, in his washing of feet, and in his surrender to and acceptance of the cross. Jesus himself described the limits of this self-emptying in this way: "No one has greater love than this, to lay down one's life for one's friends" (John 15:13). Selflessness is the very marrow of Christian holiness.

This attitude of selfless openness attacks the ego head-on, since the ego wants to control and manipulate everything and everyone within its range of influence. A selfless openness and response to whatever the present moment is asking of me, rooted in the desire to imitate the self-emptying of Jesus, incapacitates the ego and renders it powerless.

The belief that the need of the present moment is an invitation from God to forget myself and enrich the life of another is the motivating force and insight behind selfless openness. Indeed, the present moment as it unfolds before me is an expression of God's will for me. That's why this moment—and every moment—is sacred. God calls for a response in the cry of an infant, a neighbor's need, a bloated stomach in Darfur and the near extinction of an animal species.

Ideally, our selfless acts should be the blossom of an openness and response to the present moment's duty or need. An adaptable flexibility to what unfolds in the present moment made Josh's act of charity possible. However, don't be deceived; this approach can be tricky and downright risky. It demands living a life outside the confines of the ego with its constricting and exploitative obsession with what we have, what we do and what people think of us.

Far from a passive receptivity to whatever life throws my way, selfless openness calls for an alert attention to what is going on around me. It demands an awareness of what my five senses are picking up in the present circumstance and requires an active engagement with the world, especially the present moment and the situation in which I find myself.

Over the years, literally thousands of Christians, precisely because of their dedication to Christ, have leapt over the walls of the ego at a moment's notice and selflessly given of themselves for the enrichment of others. I think of Franciscan Maximilian Kolbe, a prisoner in the Auschwitz concentration camp, who freely exchanged his life for that of the condemned sergeant, husband and father Francis Gajowniczek. Soldiers returning from Iraq and Afghanistan tell stories of buddies who, at great personal risk, exposed themselves to enemy fire in order to rescue wounded comrades. On September 11, 2001, police and firefighters raced toward the collapsing Twin Towers to save people while some office workers returned to their offices to help disabled coworkers escape. Every now and then in the news, we hear stories of people whose religious commitment called them to perform heroic acts of protest so that the lives of others can be improved. These are all portraits of selfless openness and contemporary holiness.

Jill is the mother of a newborn and a two-year-old toddler. She knows only too well what it means to empty herself into the lives of her two children. On her "bad days," the self-emptying is an extraordinary challenge that tests her patience. On her "good days," she gets a feeling of liberation and ultimate satisfaction, knowing her sacrifices are literally giving life to two children. This is the kind of self-emptying that occurs in households across the world, and is another portrait of selfless openness and contemporary holiness.

THE FATHER OF ALL OF US

Abraham, "the father of all of us," to use Paul's expression (see Romans 4:16), is one of the best examples of someone actively engaged with the situation in which he found himself. At seventy-five years of age, Abraham was called by God to go beyond the comfort zone and sense of security that we can only imagine were rightfully his at such an old age. Genesis 12 gives no indication of how Abraham experienced this call from God, nor does it give any indication of what went on in his mind and heart as he and his wife gathered up their possessions to move. The chapter simply makes clear the patriarch's response: "So Abram went, as the LORD had told him" (Genesis 12:4). The letter to the Hebrews further highlights that "by faith . . . he set out, not knowing where he was going" (11:8). This self-empty-ing indicates that Abraham must have already been open and attentive to God so that, when he heard God calling him in the present moment to leave, he was ready to respond selflessly in obedience. And it certainly did not stop there.

In a most mysterious incident, Abraham's selfless response was a testimony to the agony self-emptying can sometimes en-tail. God tested the patriarch with the command, "Take your son, your only son Isaac, whom you love, and go to the land of Moriah, and offer him there as a burnt offering on one of the mountains that I shall show you" (Genesis 22:2). Again, the text does not tell us what went on within Abraham's mind and heart. All it says is, "So Abraham rose early in the morning, saddled his donkey, and took two of his young men with him, and his son Isaac; he cut the wood for the burnt offering, and set out and went to the place in the distance that God had shown him" (Genesis 22:3). He asked no questions as he responded to God's call in the present moment. The letter to the Hebrews interprets the patriarch's response as an expression of his faith (see He-brews 11:17-19). Though an angel's hand did save the life of Isaac, Abraham's obedience and selfless openness are disarm-ing and heroic.

I have met many people who have found inspiration in the story of Abraham. I think of Alex and Eileen and their mission-ary call. I first met Alex and Eileen, a retired couple from Can-ada, while teaching in a Chinese university in Beijing. Theirs is a modern-day story of Abraham and Sarah. Two years into their retirement, Alex and Eileen heard a missionary from South America preach at their Anglican church. It was not simply the missionary's words which struck them but also the valiant way he was living out his faith. As Alex and Eileen discussed what they heard that Sunday morning, something began to well up within them; they too felt oddly drawn to do what Abraham and Sarah and that missionary had done. As they talked with family and friends and their pastor, it became clear that they were being called to uproot and bring the gospel to another land. "And what better place to come to than China where you have to *live* the gospel since it is against the law for foreigners to *preach* it with their words," Eileen told me as we sipped green tea inside the Forbidden City. In their selfless openness and response to the invitation of God, Alex and Eileen have shown themselves to be worthy children of "the father of all of us."

Sally is another worthy child of Abraham. Every month she reminds me of the challenge and agony of selfless openness. She once had an amazing talent for singing. Though she never had voice lessons, she had sung in local community musicals as well as in her church choir. She relished the attention and the limelight that came with her singing. Within six months of starting spiritual direction with me, however, she began to lose her voice. She was diagnosed with Lou Gehrig's disease which, in her case, affected the muscles in her neck. Now she speaks by using a talking typewriter. I recently asked her where she finds the courage and strength to accept this disease. Echoing what must have been the spirit of Abraham, she typed a simple prayer: "Anything for you, O God. Everything for you."

The journey of faith can be challenging when the present moment calls us to uproot and move or let go of what we hold most dear or what the ego considers to be its life-support system. Such times remind us that we are more attached to self-concern, self-image, self-gratification and self-preservation than we are aware. In these moments, we can follow the example of Abraham's obedience, trusting that God is at work and that God's grace will be sufficient (see 2 Corinthians 12:9). Such selfless openness and response to God's call in this sacred moment is the essence of holiness. But beware: the ego will protest.

REFLECTION QUESTIONS

1. How would you define holiness in one sentence?

2. Which people in Scripture are models of holiness for you? Why?

3. What is God calling you to in the need or duty of *this* present moment? How are you responding to it?

3

FROM SELF-REFLECTION TO SELF-EMPTYING

The ego perceives a selfless openness and response to God's call in this sacred moment as a direct threat to its life-support system and reason for existence. Its obsession with self-concern, self-image, self-gratification and self-preservation exposes the quintessential self-absorption which sets the agenda for its action plan in life. Looking in the mirror, its every decision is based upon the answer to its one and only preoccupation: "What's in it for me?"

When a person moves beyond the ego and lives life selflessly open to God's call expressed in the duty or need of this sacred moment, they begin to experience the transformation that is called holiness. Each moment is celebrated as God invites them beyond the stranglehold of the ego by emptying themselves so that others can be enriched.

A NUANCED SHIFT IN SPIRITUAL PRACTICE
This selfless openness to the present moment requires a nu-

anced shift in our daily spiritual practices. Early on in spiritual formation, we are taught the importance of self-reflection. At day's end, the practice of self-reflection challenges us to be attentive to our sins of omission and commission as we look over the past twenty-four hours. This gives birth to contrition. It also challenges us to be attentive to the ways God has touched our lives and encouraged us to move beyond the ego, and this gives birth to humility and gratitude. Healthy self-reflection is critical for spiritual growth. However, if not properly practiced or monitored, self-reflection can devolve into scrupulosity, navel-gazing or spiritual narcissism with its fixation on one's progress or lack of progress in the spiritual life. When that happens, self-reflection becomes a stumbling block to Christian holiness.

Jesus hints at the inadequacy of self-reflection in his parable of the good Samaritan (see Luke 10:25-37). According to Jewish religious practice, priests were not allowed to touch the corpse of a stranger because it would make them ritually impure (see Leviticus 21:1-4). The priest and the Levite, perhaps thinking that the stripped and beaten man was dead—Jesus said the man had been left "half dead" (v. 30)—deliberately passed him by and left him behind. Maybe they were self-absorbed, focused on their relationship with God, and didn't want to render themselves ritually impure. The Samaritan, on the other hand, instantly responded to the need of the present moment. His deliberate act of kindness shows us that selfless openness to the present is the hallmark of holiness. "Go and do likewise" (Luke 10:37) is not only Jesus' command but also his incisive critique against any understanding of holiness that stops at self-reflection and does not include self-emptying.

Once while I was preaching a weeklong retreat, an elderly cloistered nun in the community asked to speak with me privately. Once we got together, she proceeded to tell me about her spiritual life and her relationship with Jesus. For over forty-five minutes, she used words to paint a very detailed landscape of her soul and the many spiritual gifts she had received during her fifty-plus years in the monastery. Upon finishing, she looked at me and asked, "So, Father, after all these years of fidelity, wouldn't you say that I have done pretty well for myself?"

I shifted in my chair and looked away. Though I had no doubt that God had clearly touched this woman over a lifetime, I was extraordinarily uncomfortable at how much time and energy she had spent in self-reflection—or perhaps I should say self-absorption. I looked at her and very gingerly replied, "Does anyone really care?"

Her shoulders slumped as her face turned red. I continued, "Sister, though God might have done great things for you, the important thing is what you are doing for God and for your community. Are you growing in selflessness and unconditional love?"

With my question asked, she very politely ended our conversation and shuffled into the chapel.

Though forms of self-reflection are important in spiritual formation, especially for beginners, there comes a point when a Christian disciple has to move beyond self-reflection and begin to focus on others and their needs. "Me" begins to disappear as an initial point of reference as I forget myself and, in imitation of Jesus, become interested in enriching the lives of others. The focus of attention and concern changes and becomes decidedly outward, not inward. The ego's mirrors are transformed into windows. This is the meaning of the self-emptying mentioned in Philippians 2:7 and is the practical expression of love.

THE PRACTICAL CONSEQUENCES

Mary of Nazareth is an example of someone whose inclination

was to selflessly respond to the present moment and empty herself without counting the cost or weighing the egotistical concerns of the self-absorbed. God's invitation to her to be the mother of Jesus was an incredible offer. With her selfless openness and "yes," Mary instantly went from maiden to mother.

We fail to remember, however, the tremendous blow to her ego that was at the root of such a response. In a culture where women were second-class citizens and had few rights and priv-ileges, her reputation was one of the few things she could claim for herself and protect. And now she was pregnant—and un-married. The gossip quickly spread. Word traveled through the hill country and reached the ears of her cousin Elizabeth (see Luke 1:43). It also reached the ears of Joseph, to whom she was engaged. His initial reaction, suggestive of his strong religious values (Matthew's Gospel refers to him as "righteous") and maybe even a self-absorbed concern, was to quietly dismiss her (see Matthew 1:19). Then Joseph was told in a dream that Mary's pregnancy was an action of God and that he should take her as his wife. Matthew succinctly records his selfless response which is as magnanimous as his future wife's: "When Joseph awoke from sleep, he did as the angel of the Lord commanded him" (1:24). Though he was perhaps riddled with questions, he asked none of them. Mary's and Joseph's selfless openness and response to God's call in their sacred moment enriched the his-tory of humanity with the birth of Jesus, the savior and re-deemer of the world.

We also see the practical consequences of self-emptying in the life of Paul of Tarsus. Paul gives us good reason to believe that before his conversion to Christianity, he was self-reflective and maybe self-absorbed: focused on the law and how he was living it. As a matter of fact, he described himself "as to the law, a Pharisee . . . as to righteousness under the law, blameless" (Philippians 3:5-6). However, the advice he gave the Christian community at Corinth (see 1 Corinthians 8:1–11:1) shows that, over time, he clearly moved from self-reflection to self-emptying, expressed in an extraordinary sensitivity to others.

It appears that the Corinthian community asked Paul to answer three questions which had arisen in their everyday lives: Could members of the community eat the meat bought in the marketplace even though they knew, as was typical of so much food in the city of Corinth, it was originally offered in sacrifice at a pagan temple? Could Christians accept invitations to dinners held in banquet rooms of pagan temples where a sacrificial libation to the god was present? Could Christians accept invitations to dinner in the homes of unbelievers?

Paul's response to these questions comes out of his unique understanding of the freedom that comes in Christ Jesus. For Paul, individual freedom is never expressed in isolation. Rather, it finds its most authentic expression in relationship to the larger community and when it is subordinate to the obligation of mutual charity. Furthermore, Christian freedom is not a freedom *from* restrictions and restraints where the ego's whims, wishes, passions and desires are pursued and indulged. On the contrary, it is a freedom from the ego which finds expression in a life *for* others. "For though I am free with respect to all," Paul says, "I have made myself a slave to all, so that I might win more of them" (1 Corinthians 9:19). Christ sets us free from the ego to live a life for the enrichment of others.

From this perspective, Paul offers a succinct summary of his answer to the community's questions, expressed first negatively and then positively, rooted in his own imitation of the selflessness and self-emptying of Christ:

So, whether you eat or drink, or whatever you do, do everything for the glory of God. Give no offense to Jews or to Greeks or to the church of God, just as I try to please everyone in everything I do, not seeking my own advantage, but that of many, so that they may be saved. Be imitators of me, as I am of Christ. (1 Corinthians 10:31–11:1)

Paul reminds the Corinthians to move beyond self-absorption and self-concern—"not seeking my own advantage"—and to think in terms of the group—"but that of many." And he presents the self-emptying of Christ as the example par excellence.

Selfless openness to God's call in this sacred moment replaces the mirrors in our lives with windows. It reflects the self-emptying of Christ at his birth and in his death. It paves the path to freedom from the ego. But seeing clearly through the windows and finding the path of freedom require knowing how God calls.

REFLECTION QUESTONS

1. When has your preoccupation with self-concern, self-image, self-gratification and self-preservation hindered you from responding to God's call? What did you think or feel was at stake?

2. What forms of self-reflection do you practice on a regular basis? When are they helpful? When are they unhelpful?

3. What practical steps can you take to change the center of attention from yourself to others?

4

HOW GOD CALLS

*F*or over a month, in all his devotional and spiritual reading, Phil kept seeing the word *forgiveness*. At first he thought it was a strange coincidence that this word kept appearing seemingly out of nowhere, in different books he was reading and then even one Sunday when his pastor preached on forgiving and moving on.

As the days went by and he reflected on his life, Phil realized that he needed to mend fences with his good friend whom he hadn't talked to after an unfortunate misunderstanding eight months earlier. He began to believe that the constantly emerging theme of forgiveness was God's invitation to make a phone call. In picking up the phone and dialing his friend's number, Phil was selflessly responding to God's call in the sacred moment. And without knowing it, Phil was coming one step closer to overcoming the ego and developing the habit of self-emptying for the sake of others.

THUNDER AND LIGHTNING
Phil's experience is delightfully ordinary and a good reminder

that the call of God comes into our lives in a variety of ways—
one of which is through the noticable and dramatic.

There is a strong scriptural tradition which suggests that the
divine presence commands attention with striking displays of
fire, wind, thunder, lightning and earthquakes (see Exodus
19:16; 20:18; Deuteronomy 4:11; 5:22-24; Judges 5:4-5; Psalm
18:11-15; 68:7-8; Isaiah 30:27; Nahum 1:3-5). Indeed, sometimes
when God calls, the heavens break open and God's message,
like a thunderbolt shaking up the sky, reverberates in the ears
of the spiritually mature who listen. Extraordinary experiences, whether visions or spiritual locutions when a person
hears the voice of God in the heart or in dreams, are sometimes
the channels of God's invitation. These events can shake us up
and dazzle us as if they were a divine fireworks display. Such
moments have an expressed other-worldliness and divine obviousness to them.

The apostle Paul's experience as described in the Acts of the
Apostles is the classic example (see 9:4-9; 22:6-11; 26:12-18). Paul
had been making a name for himself as the persecutor of the
Christians. And then something happened to him on the road to
Damascus that pulled the carpet from underneath his feet. The
call of the risen Christ in the present moment challenged him to
do an about-face. The persecutor of the Christians suddenly became the preeminent preacher of Jesus Christ par excellence.
The lasting effect of Paul's drama upon his everyday life clearly
indicates the authenticity of the divine call.

Melanie still remembers the exact Sunday some seven years
ago when she was singing a hymn in church and her life changed
in an instant. As she sang, she heard an interior voice say to her,
"I love you so much. Don't you want to give me something?"
Melanie said the moment felt like an earthquake which opened
up a fault line deep within her soul. She was overcome with

tears. Reflecting on the experience, she told me, "I realized at that very moment that God had given me a million dollars. I had given him back twenty-five cents. And I thought we were even." Her selfless openness and response to that sacred moment has set her on a journey of daily prayer and volunteering at a women's counseling center. In imitation of the self-emptying of Jesus, she is enriching the lives of others.

I've had my own powerful instances of hearing God speak. As long as I can remember, I've had a fascination with China, the Chinese people and the Chinese language. My deceased mother used to tell the story of how, at a very young age, I would go in the backyard of our New Orleans home with a shovel and a glass of iced tea and start digging a hole. When asked what I was doing, I would reply, "I'm going to China!" But I would always abandon the project for lack of a bigger shovel and more iced tea.

I remember the afternoon in September 1991 when I received a form letter from the head of the Franciscan Order in Rome. The letter had been sent to all seventeen thousand Franciscans in the world and expressed a need for volunteers to learn the Chinese language and culture and then take the Franciscan presence back to mainland China after a hiatus of more than fifty years. Though I was in the midst of a blossoming preaching ministry, I knew that I had to respond to the request. Still, I hesitated because of my poor linguistic ability. However, a few days after the letter arrived, I had a dream in which I found myself in a Chinese library and was able to read all the titles of the books. I bolted up in bed and said to myself, "It's time to volunteer." I finally made it to China in 1992—not through a self-made tunnel but via United Airlines—and ended up staying there as a missionary for eleven-and-a-half years.

Such dramatic calls by God speak volumes about how God

intervenes in sometimes remarkable ways in the lives of ordinary people. Those experiences are like being hit by lightning; life is never the same. However, as I remind people time and time again in spiritual direction, these types of calls from God are the rare exception. I sometimes think they are given to hard-headed people who are set in their ways and who are not familiar with any other way that God can speak. To be attentive only to the dramatic is to potentially miss other ways that God issues a call or reveals a required duty or unmet need in this sacred moment.

A SOFT WHISPER

Two stories in the Hebrew Scriptures suggest that the call of God is not always as spectacular, extraordinary or obvious as one might think. The first is the famous incident of Elijah at the cave of Mt. Horeb (see 1 Kings 19:11-18). The Lord told Elijah to stand on Mt. Horeb and said that the Lord would pass by. After each natural occurrence of a strong wind, an earthquake and fire, the Scriptures state explicitly "but the LORD was not in [it]" (see vv. 11-12). And then comes the telling verse: "and after the fire a sound of sheer silence" (v. 12). Sometimes rendered "the sound of a soft whisper," the silence is precisely what prompts Elijah, believing that no one can see God and live (see Genesis 32:30; Exodus 33:20; Judges 6:22; 13:22; Isaiah 6:5), to cover his face. This passage suggests that the divine presence can sometimes be wrapped in something barely perceptible to the human senses.

In addition to Elijah's experience, Samuel's call to prophesy suggests that God's voice is not always as clearly recognizable as we might assume (see 1 Samuel 3:1-14). Even as a young priest who ministered under Eli, Samuel still needed to learn how to discern the voice of God. Three times God called Samuel by name, and each time he mistook the voice for Eli's. It was Eli who first realized that God was calling Samuel. And so Eli advised the young boy, "Go, lie down; and if he calls you, you shall say, 'Speak, LORD, for your servant is listening'" (v. 9). Young Samuel followed the advice and received the prophetic call.

These two stories from the Hebrew Scriptures simply anticipate what would be dramatically expressed at Bethlehem: God's word is spoken *in* and *through* human experience. What makes it extraordinary is that it is expressed through the ordinary. There is a physicality and this-worldly quality about God's call. God chooses to use ordinary events, human people, and sometimes our deepest hunches and gut feelings to speak to us. This was certainly Phil's experience as he kept bumping into the word *forgiveness* in his reading and subsequently made the connection that God was calling him to reconcile with a good friend. Human experience is the megaphone through which God issues a call or reveals a duty or need. It can be as ordinary and surprising as a polite knock on the door.

REFLECTION QUESTIONS

1. Have you had a dramatic experience of God's call? If so, what were the circumstances surrounding it? What emotional reaction did it call forth from you?

2. When has God spoken to you through a hunch or gut feeling? What did it lead you to do?

3. How do you know when God is speaking to you through your ordinary, daily experience? What does God's voice sound like?

5

THE KNOCK ON THE DOOR

*T*he call of God is like a knock on the door of the present moment in which we find ourselves: the blank stare of a relative with Alzheimer's disease, the niggling self-concern when an addiction is developing, a deep attraction or abiding desire to do a good deed that seems to come out of nowhere, the tears of those left behind by a natural disaster such as a tornado, a word of advice or encouragement given by a spouse or trusted friend, a restlessness that is never satisfied and yearns for something more, a committed relationship that is suddenly turning sour, a coincidence that remains in the forefront of our awareness, an outstretched hand on the street, a child's hurt feelings, an opportunity of a lifetime. Our response to such knocks shows just how close we are to God and holiness.

Caroline comes regularly for spiritual direction. She told me how she had applied for and received multiple copies of her children's birth certificates. After picking them up, she ran a few errands. That evening she discovered that she had misplaced the birth certificates. As she was making a phone call, she realized the severity of such a loss. If those birth certificates got into the wrong hands, her children's identities could be stolen. She was frantic and searched high and low for the lost certificates. After two days passed without her finding them, in a moment of desperation she fell to her knees and begged for God's help. During that prayer, she remembered that, while doing her errands, she had stopped at a coffee shop for some bottled water. Perhaps she had accidentally left the birth certificates there. The following morning while on her way to a meeting, she stopped at the coffee shop and found the birth certificates waiting for her behind the cash register. Ecstatic and relieved, she thanked the employees profusely and offered each a small reward.

A customer was watching this entire scene play out. As Caroline was leaving the coffee shop to go to her meeting, the man said, "Miss, you must live a really lucky life." Though Caroline needed to get to her meeting, she took the time to walk over to the man's table. She replied, "I don't know if I live a lucky life but I sure try to live a godly life. And God seems to be constantly replying with blessings upon me."

"I've pretty much given up on God," the customer replied. "He doesn't bless me. I lost my retirement in the recent economic crisis. My daughter got divorced last year, lost her job and is now studying for another master's degree. I promised her that I would pay for it. I am also caring for her two children. Like I said, you must have a lucky life."

Caroline reminded the man that it is important in difficult times to have an ongoing relationship with God. "That's what has always helped me to get through the tough and trying times in my own life," she said. She told him that she was recently diagnosed with breast cancer and was just doing what the doctors recommended and trusting God.

Caroline could see the man's face and demeanor change. A

faint glint was appearing in his eyes. The man said, "You know, Miss, I don't come to this coffee shop often. Actually, this is only my third time in about two months. But for some strange reason, I felt summoned here today, and for the life of me, I didn't know why. But now I know. The loss of your birth certificates brought you here—and maybe I felt drawn here—so you could come into my life and remind me of the importance of trusting God and leading a godly life."

SURPRISE!

God knocks on the door of this sacred moment as it unfolds before us. Unfortunately, we are often unaware of that knock until we look back and reflect on an experience in hindsight. God's knock can be as soft as an intuition or a gut feeling; it can be as loud as a need to which only we can respond. Sometimes that knock surprises even the most spiritually attuned among us.

God's knock, expressed in the need of the present moment, might have surprised Jesus as he walked in the district of Tyre and Sidon (see Matthew 15:21-28). Jesus seems to have had the understanding that his mission was only to the Jews. He himself said, "I was sent only to the lost sheep of the house of Israel" (Matthew 15:24). And so, when a Canaanite woman pleaded with Jesus to cure her demon-tormented daughter, Jesus initially refused and coldly replied, "It is not fair to take the children's food and throw it to the dogs" (v. 26). However, the Canaanite woman's reply that even the dogs get to eat scraps that fall from the table, as well as the unmet need of the sacred moment, was enough to expand Jesus' sense of mission to include this non-Jew.

OPENING THE DOOR

Later in Jesus' life, in the garden of Gethsemane, we see Jesus truly struggling to accept and surrender to God's knock in the present moment. It is another example of Jesus having to deal with a request that might have caught him off-guard. Luke's description of Jesus' sweat being like drops of blood speaks to the enormous interior struggle going on within Jesus' heart and soul (see Luke 22:44). And yet we once again see Jesus make the great breakthrough from self-reflection to self-emptying as he prays, "Father, if you are willing, remove this cup from me; yet, not my will but yours be done" (Luke 22:42). Later, as he breathes his last, we see his total self-emptying for the enrichment of others as he prays, "Father, into your hands I commend my spirit" (Luke 23:46).

These events in the life of Jesus remind us that holiness begins with a selfless openness to this sacred moment and ends with a self-emptying response to God's call expressed in the present required duty or unmet need before us. That's the simplicity of it, but therein lies the challenge: to be attuned to our surroundings—attuned to God's knock—and willing to respond to what our senses are registering. This was the liberating insight in the lives of people like Abraham, Mary and Joseph, Jesus, Paul, and a multitude of witnesses who have gone before us. God is always knocking on the door of our experience—just as God did in the coffee shop with Caroline and the stranger who felt hopeless—and selfless openness means we live in imitation of Jesus with one hand on the doorknob ready and willing to take the time to open it.

WHEN DID WE SEE YOU?

Jesus' parable about the judgment of the nations (see Matthew 25:31-46) suggests that the very presence of God is in the duty or need of the moment; that's why every moment is truly sacred. At the final judgment, the Son of Man will separate hu-

manity as a shepherd does the sheep and goats. The sheep—
who are the righteous—will take the place of honor on his
right. And why are they there? Because they responded to the
needs of the Son of Man: "For I was hungry and you gave me
food, I was thirsty and you gave me something to drink, I was
a stranger and you welcomed me, I was naked and you gave me
clothing, I was sick and you took care of me, I was in prison
and you visited me" (vv. 35-36).

The righteous respond with embarrassment and surprise.
They ask, almost in disbelief and fearing the Son of Man is mis-
taken, "When did we see you hungry, thirsty, a stranger, naked,
sick or in prison?" And the Son of Man replies by painting a
picture of the essence of holiness, the challenge of self-emptying and the importance of selfless openness to God's call in this
sacred moment: "Truly I tell you, just as you did it to one of the
least of these who are members of my family, you did it to me"
(v. 40). To open the door to any knock in our lives is to welcome
the presence of God.

The point is obvious: the righteous inherit eternal life not
because they *see* the Lord everywhere—by their own admission, they didn't! Rather, they inherit it because they are attuned to their surroundings and selflessly respond to the needs
at hand even though they are unaware of the sacredness of this
moment. In their selfless response that enriches the lives of
others, they are, in effect, answering the call of God expressed
in the physicality of this world's duties and needs.

I have witnessed just such a response. As a young priest in
the mid-1980s, I was living at a Catholic church in the Bronx
while doing doctoral studies at Fordham University. Because of
its large congregation, the church had four full-time priests. As
a priest-in-residence, I was happy to help out when there was a
need.

I remember that the evening news typically opened with the latest information about a strange fatal disease that was affecting homosexual men. It seemed to have started in California but now had moved to New York. At that time it wasn't called AIDS, and no one knew how it was being spread. Extreme caution was used around anyone who was affected.

A telephone call came into the rectory. It was the father of a twenty-year-old man named Doug. Doug had contracted this strange disease and was asking for a visit by a priest. Monsignor Henry, the pastor in his seventies, asked all three full-time priests to go; each refused, using the severity and unknown cause of the disease as an excuse. Monsignor Henry then approached me. I was hesitant and was going to use my studies as an excuse. However, when he agreed to accompany me, I decided to go.

Once we arrived at the hospital, we were told to put on protective "moon suits" before going in to Doug's room. He looked much older and sicker than I had expected. We talked softly for about fifteen minutes; then Doug began to cry.

"What's wrong, Doug?" I asked.

He looked at me and with incredible sadness replied, "It dawns on me that no one has even touched me in over three months."

I let those words sink in and wondered how I would have handled life without a handshake or hug for three months. As I thought about that, I suddenly became aware of Monsignor Henry slowly removing the helmet and garb of the protective "moon suit." And then I witnessed the parable of the judgment of the nations played out as elderly Monsignor Henry bent over and hugged dying Doug.

A holy silence descended upon the room. I wondered how Monsignor Henry could be willing to risk his own life by responding to Doug that way.

We drove home in virtual silence. As we approached the church in the Bronx, I turned to Monsignor Henry, but before I could say a word he simply said with tears in his eyes, "Years ago, I told Jesus that I would give him everything—and I mean *everything*. Today, I was able to give to Jesus what he has given to me." Monsignor Henry subconsciously knew that selfless openness could lead to an encounter with the God who empties himself in the ordinary yet sacred moment before him.

The world and the present situation in which we find ourselves take on a luminous quality as we grow in the awareness that they are the place for an encounter with God. Yet, though there is often a physicality to it, God's call can still be easily missed because of its subtlety or misinterpreted because of human expectations about how God should speak or what God's will is. That's why it's important to have a proper understanding of God's will and a reliable practice of discernment.

REFLECTION QUESTIONS

1. When was the last time God knocked on the door of your experience? How did you respond?

2. When were you caught off-guard by God's call? How did you respond?

3. Which spiritual practices can help you selflessly respond to the poor, the sick and the marginalized? What obstacles or prejudices do you need to overcome to be selflessly open to them?

6

A NEW UNDERSTANDING

OF GOD'S WILL

For the vast majority of my life, I understood God's will for me as something that had already been predetermined. For example, I thought that on the day of my conception, God decided the role that I was going to play in the history of salvation. And then I assumed I was supposed to spend the early part of my life "picking God's brain" in order to figure out what God wanted me to do. I'd think, *Hopefully, I correctly discerned the vocation in life God intended for me—though I won't know if I got it right or not, of course, until the day I die and meet my Maker.*

Over the years, I have gradually become uncomfortable with this understanding of God's will. The problem is that it smacks of the pagan notion of fate: Everything has been predetermined for me. My eternal happiness is not based upon my freely chosen response to the grace of God in my life but rather on whether or not I managed to correctly guess my vocation and role in God's plan of salvation history.

GOD'S WILL REVEALED

There is another way of understanding God's will that dates
back to the earliest days of Christianity. Inserted within the
letter to the Colossians is an ancient Christian hymn that sings
of the primacy and preeminence of Christ in creation. It is
worth quoting in full:

> [Christ] is the image of the invisible God, the firstborn of all
> creation; for in him all things in heaven and on earth were
> created, things visible and invisible, whether thrones or do-
> minions or rulers or powers—all things have been created
> through him and for him. He himself is before all things, and
> in him all things hold together. He is the head of the body,
> the church; he is the beginning, the firstborn from the dead,
> so that he might come to have first place in everything. For
> in him all the fullness of God was pleased to dwell, and
> through him God was pleased to reconcile to himself all
> things, whether on earth or in heaven, by making peace
> through the blood of his cross. (Colossians 1:15-20)

According to this hymn, Christ stands center stage in creation. Everything came into existence through Christ and
everything exists for him. Alienated creation comes back into
harmony with God and is "reconciled" through Christ's self-
emptying on the cross—his selfless openness and response to
the sacred moment. In this cosmic vision of creation, Christ
has absolute preeminence as the focal point of reconciliation; in
the words of the letter to the Ephesians, "[God] has made
known to us the mystery of his will, according to his good pleasure that he set forth in Christ, as a plan for the fullness of time,
to gather up all things in him, things in heaven and things on
earth" (Ephesians 1:9-10).

And so the will of God is that, as history plays itself out and winds down, all creation is woven together through the redemptive warp and woof of Christ. This tapestry culminates in the kingdom of God and the lordship of Jesus Christ.

In light of this divine will, God deliberately loves me into existence with "divine reckless passion," as a friend calls it, and desires that my decisions and actions help realize the lordship of Christ right where I am. This is a choice that is always set before me. And this is where my selfless openness and response to God's call in this sacred moment come into play. This is what holiness is all about: Every time I freely choose to imitate Christ by emptying myself and enriching the life of another, I help promote the full realization of the kingdom and the lordship of Christ.

COWORKERS AND AMBASSADORS

Years ago while doing research in Italy, I met a missionary to Africa. He was studying a very primitive tribe which had an almost mystical connection to the primal element of fire. This missionary told me how a fire was always burning in the middle of the tribal village. To lose the fire was tantamount to losing the very heart of the tribe. Every year, right before the rainy season began, the elders of this tribe would gather together and choose four members to become "keepers of the flame." During the driving afternoon rains, these four tribesmen had the sole task and responsibility of preserving a lit fire in their huts.

That is a good analogy for the role that the baptized play in the kingdom of God. Like contemporary "keepers of the flame," Christians are challenged to preserve and promote Christ's lordship over all creation in every single moment in which we find ourselves. We do that by self-emptying, not by self-reflection. Knowing that our ordinary, everyday experience is the place where God issues a call, we focus our attention upon this sacred moment and ask how we can respond, in imitation of Christ, with a selfless openness and self-emptying, thus enriching the lives of others. As we do so, we become "co-workers for the kingdom of God" (Colossians 4:11). We also become "ambassadors"—"a person who acts as a representative or promoter of a specified activity," according to the *Concise Oxford American Dictionary*—for Christ (see 2 Corinthians 5:20).

Years ago, I lived with a Franciscan priest by the name of DePaul. By day, he was an administrator in a theology school. By night, however, long after the sun set, he would walk the dimly lit streets of Chicago's seedier neighborhoods and befriend prostitutes. He became the confidant and counselor of many. And when one of his lady friends was ready to leave her pimp and prostitution and begin a new life, DePaul had a network of people in St. Louis ready and willing to help the woman with the training and skills needed to do just that.

I was intrigued by DePaul's nighttime ministry and asked to accompany him one evening. The following afternoon, I had an opportunity to debrief the experience with DePaul. After I shared my impressions and reactions, he spoke passionately about how he felt he was doing what Jesus did in his own openness to public sinners and the marginalized of society. "There's really nothing glamorous about what I do," he said. "I just try to respond to the emotional needs of the woman before me. I keep asking myself, 'What would Jesus do for this woman and how would he do it?' In responding to those questions, I like to believe I am helping this woman feel connected to God's love and hope for her." In a very practical way, by imitating Jesus' selfless openness and response to a prostitute's emotional need, DePaul became a coworker for the kingdom and an ambassador for Christ.

As coworkers for the kingdom and ambassadors for Christ,

we are sent on mission to this sacred moment before us. DePaul would later remind me, "A Christian without a sense of mission is a stunted Christian." We need to ask ourselves: What does the commitment to Christ challenge us to do right where we are? How can we preserve and promote Christ's lordship right here, right now? What would the kingdom of God look like in this particular situation? What is the required duty or unmet need of this sacred moment and how would Jesus respond to it? The answer to these questions is God's call and requires the daily practice of ongoing discernment.

REFLECTION QUESTIONS

1. How do you understand God's will? What role do Christians play in that understanding?

2. How does God's desire for the kingdom to reign and the lordship of Jesus Christ to be known affect your life and the decisions that you make? When have you found God's desire inconvenient or unacceptable?

3. How does a sense of mission influence your daily actions and decisions?

7

PRINCIPLES OF ONGOING
DISCERNMENT

*C*hristians traditionally understand discernment as the practice and ability to hear God's call in major life decisions such as one's vocation or marriage partner. It includes the spiritual knack of knowing and distinguishing between God's call and the ego's desire. Essentially, it's faith-based decision making. And its result is expansive and gives a definite and defining direction to our lives—sometimes even a change of direction. I refer to this as "commitment discernment," or Discernment with a capital *D*.

There is another kind of discernment which I call "ongoing discernment." Think of it as discernment with a small *d*. It is less of a specific practice and more of a daily attitude and orientation that permeates my everyday routine. Like a pair of glasses, it corrects the vision that my ego, with its obsession with self-concern, self-image, self-gratification and self-preservation, brings to every situation. And similar to a computer program, it is always running in the background of my life. Unlike commitment discernment, which occurs at a crossroads in life and has the drama of a drumroll associated with it, ongoing discernment occurs at a stoplight and has Muzak playing in the background. It is constantly assessing this sacred moment and scanning for answers to the age-old questions "What would Jesus do and how would he do it?" And it is based upon three important principles.

BUILDING BLOCKS OF THE KINGDOM

The duties and responsibilities of my present state in life are the basic building blocks for the kingdom of God. This first principle reminds me that in virtually every situation, nothing is more important than the duties of my present state in life. Good decisions, freely and wisely made in good faith, lay the foundation for the lordship of Jesus Christ in my life. Even past decisions and past actions, crippled by human weakness or repented of due to deliberate sin, can be woven into the tapestry of redemption by my decision to be faithful in the present to the duties and responsibilities that are their consequences. Far from an inconvenience, the cry of an infant, the pressures of making an adequate income for family support and the loneliness felt on a Friday night all become places where God's call to holiness is tested and forged, and where the building blocks of the kingdom of God can be laid.

Michelle and her two sisters used to take turns caring daily for their elderly mother, who had been widowed for many years. Michelle once confided to me in a spiritual direction session that her husband was considering applying for a new position which would entail their move to another city. Though excited about the opportunity, Michelle felt nervous about losing the connection with her mother and about the added burden the move would place on her two sisters. Over a period of three months, as she prayed over her situation with an attitude of ongoing discernment, Michelle saw that she and her husband needed to stay in town. She even began thinking about asking her elderly mother to move in with her, which would give her mother a sense of stability and security she didn't enjoy at the time. It also seemed like a natural consequence of caring for an aging parent. After discussing the idea with her husband, Michelle invited her mother into their home. Though it entailed some major readjustments for Michelle and her husband, their selfless openness and response to the required duty of the moment was a wonderful testimony to the mother-daughter bond—and to the kingdom of God.

We sometimes underestimate the present situation as the place of God's call and the foundation where the building blocks for the kingdom can be laid. The ego, with its fixation upon self-image and self-preservation, is always looking elsewhere for the more exotic or heroic place—and sometimes the easier, less stressful place—to become holy. Under a pious pretext, the ego insinuates that we simply cannot become holy in our present situation, that our current duties and responsibilities distract and sidetrack us from promoting the lordship of Jesus Christ.

"Retreat and restart" is one of the most tempting scams in the ego's version of spiritual formation. The ego tells us to pack our bags and head somewhere else—to retreat from our present situation and start afresh in a new and different place or occupation or circumstance that guarantees instant holiness. It seduces us with the illusion that there is a magical quarry somewhere else where the building blocks for the kingdom can be found.

The truth is, the cornerstone of the kingdom is found in *this* sacred moment. It is formed from the imitation of Christ by which we witness to his lordship: to empty ourselves for the benefit of another. That's why any and every situation holds the grace for the transformation called holiness. We can become holy right where we are.

Of course, sometimes our present circumstance is based upon past decisions which were forced upon us and not freely made. Or perhaps we or the other person did not fully understand the implications and consequences of our decisions when we made them. Decisions might have been made in haste or in isolation, without the wisdom of those who know us best. They might have been shrouded in deception, either on our part or on the part of another, or been made with an immature, overly emotional investment in self-concern, self-image, self-gratification and self-preservation. Such decisions can sometimes give birth to a situation that is debilitating, unhealthy, abusive, dangerous or downright life-threatening. In order to discover the building blocks of the kingdom and how to selflessly respond to God's call in this sacred moment, we might have to enter into the spiritual practice of commitment discernment. In some rare cases, our duties and responsibilities might change or be redirected due to a renegotiation of our present state in life. However, this is the exception rather than the rule.

A HEALTHY LIFESTYLE

The second principle of ongoing discernment is that *holiness is oriented toward a healthy lifestyle*. There is a common misconception that God's call will always be challenging, undesirable and personally repugnant. As a spiritual directee once said to me, "I am always inclined to think it is the call of God when a situation requires me to be a 'doormat for Jesus' where people can wipe their feet." Though God's call can sting, especially when it challenges the ego's self-centered agenda, it never leads to a lifestyle that is unhealthy or personally debilitating and destructive.

Selfless openness and self-emptying require tact, sensitivity to one's own emotional needs and sometimes diplomacy. Though I am not a psychologist and do not want to over-psychologize, I will say that healthy Christians are only too aware that they cannot give what they do not have. Consequently, they pay attention to the important issues of their physical health: sleep, food, exercise and leisure. They also pay attention to important issues of emotional health and psychological stability: laughter, healthy personal boundaries, rightly ordered priorities, personal friendships, vacations and daily forms of healthy escapes. Healthy Christians know that God's call in this sacred moment can sometimes be for the enrichment of *themselves*—so that they can be prepared and ready tomorrow for the enrichment of others. Selfless openness and self-emptying are spiritual virtues, not psychological neuroses.

THE FAMILY AFFAIR

Ongoing discernment requires a commitment to a church community. This third principle reminds me that Christian holiness is not a solitary, individualistic affair. It is impossible for a Christian "to be spiritual, but not religious," meaning that he or she does not have regular contact with a Christian community. The kingdom of God involves nothing less than all creation being reunited and reconciled under the lordship of Jesus Christ; it is *the* family affair par excellence. As an active member of a Christian community, I am reminded of my wider obligations and responsibilities for the kingdom. Through Sunday worship and the church's mission outreach, I am challenged to experience the height and depth, the breadth and width of God's reconciling will.

Ongoing discernment is amplified through dialogue and discussion with family, friends and other members of this Christian community. On the other hand, ongoing discernment that is doggedly independent, that winces at the wisdom of the community, or that intentionally ignores church documents or pastoral statements of church leadership expresses a privatized, individualistic faith which could potentially lose its Christian character. I share this sacred moment with theologians and saints who have gone before me in the past and with bishops, priests, pastors, ministers and spiritual companions who journey with me in the present. My selfless openness and response to God's call enjoys consultation and dialogue with these people and does not fear them.

Sam is an elder in his church. For over a year, he had been feeling a strange attraction toward community outreach. But he wasn't quite sure how to translate this attraction into action. In discussions with his wife, he mentioned that getting involved in local politics might be one way to satisfy his attraction and growing interest. His wife raised the issue of whether or not that would be realistic, considering his full-time job as a dentist and his responsibilities at home and church.

Sam continued thinking and praying over this attraction and brought it to his spiritual direction sessions. He clearly sensed a call from God but didn't know how to respond to it. He also brought the issue to the council of elders and to the senior pastor of his church. They reminded him that the church was looking for a way to serve the local community. After discussion, they asked Sam to organize a church committee to investigate the possibility of establishing a food pantry, a homeless shelter or a soup kitchen for the local community. He was excited about this opportunity as he continued to pray over his emerging attraction to community outreach and the possible action God was calling him to.

An awareness of the three principles of ongoing discernment helped Sam narrow his focus and sense more specifically God's call to him in this sacred moment. But awareness is not enough when it comes to ongoing discernment. We also need to learn to incorporate some of its practices.

REFLECTION QUESTIONS

1. When have you been tempted to retreat from present obligations and duties and restart in a new environment? What changed your mind?

2. How does a personally healthy lifestyle help to promote God's kingdom and the lordship of Jesus Christ over creation? What's the difference between healthy selfishness and neurotic selflessness?

3. What role does the institutional church play in your own practice of ongoing discernment?

8

PRACTICES OF ONGOING DISCERNMENT

*P*eople sometimes ask me to describe a method of ongoing discernment. That request always puts me in an awkward position. I find myself hesitating to offer a precise, systematic technique. After all, ongoing discernment is a bit slippery and vague; a method for it is something that is talked around but cannot be precisely pinned down and described. I usually respond with the most basic explanation: "It's trying to answer and respond to the two questions in every situation in which I find myself: *What would Jesus do and how would he do it?*" Unfortunately, the answer usually raises more questions.

Ongoing discernment as a spiritual practice is more intuitive and less systematic than some people are comfortable with. Its goal is the awareness of and attention to the present moment since this is the time and place where we encounter the call of God. Jesus often spoke of the importance of this goal in his teachings and parables, such as when he warned, "Keep awake . . . for you do not know on what day your Lord is coming"

(Matthew 24:42; see also Matthew 24:45–25:13; 25:31-46). Paul picks up on the importance of this kind of vigilance too (see 1 Thessalonians 5:6), as does the book of Revelation (see Revelation 16:15). Three practices of ongoing discernment betray its imprecise nature and help to foster the goal of watchfulness.

PRAYER

Daily, consistent prayer is the first practice of ongoing discernment. This practice is not so much about "saying prayers" as it is about fostering and fueling the awareness of the closeness and call of God in my everyday, ordinary routine. Prayer should make me prayerful—that is, it should help me be attentive to the many ways that God speaks to me not only in prayer but also *after* prayer, as I load the dishwasher, pack my school bag, drive to work, monitor the children on the playground, balance the checkbook and prepare the evening meal. In other words, my daily devotional time should drain into my daily activity. Praying with Scripture and the examen (two practices that I will describe in the next two chapters), centering prayer, meditation, praying with a rosary, prayers of petition, and intercession are all ways to grow in the spirit of watchfulness and vigilance.

The parable of the widow and the unjust judge highlights the effects of a daily, consistent prayer life (see Luke 18:1-8). In it, a widow continually appears before a judge seeking justice from her opponent. The judge keeps refusing. Finally, he decides to rule on the case, saying to himself, "Though I have no fear of God and no respect for anyone, yet because this widow keeps bothering me, I will grant her justice, so that she may not wear me out by continually coming" (vv. 4-5). Luke interprets this story as "a parable about [the disciples'] need to pray always and not . . . lose heart" (v. 1).

Many people understand Luke's interpretation in a way that gives me cause to question: Is God really like an unjust judge whom we have to nag and persistently hound to get a hearing or an answer? That certainly has not been my experience of God. And doesn't God know what we want even before we ask? Our faith tradition has continually stated that God is omniscient and knows all our needs and wants.

The creative beauty of Jesus' parables is that they can have different interpretations. After all, they were meant to be heard and interpreted by each individual listener from his or her own life situation and experience. And so, if we take a second look at the parable with a different pair of glasses, another interpretation emerges: God is the ignored, marginalized widow who has no rights, and God is asking *us* to give justice to those seeking it!

If God's call comes in our ordinary, everyday experience, then we persistently and confidently pray in order to hear *what God is asking us to do!* This certainly gives us a deeper appreciation for Jesus' words to the righteous in the parable of the judgment of the nations: "for I was hungry and you gave me food, I was thirsty and you gave me something to drink, I was a stranger and you welcomed me" (Matthew 25:35). Again, holiness is imitating Jesus in this sacred moment by selfless openness and self-emptying for the enrichment of others.

As we grow in awareness of and attention to the present moment through daily, consistent prayer, we discover that selfless openness and self-emptying for the sake of others sometimes require inaction, ironically. A valid interpretation of the parable of the talents suggests this (see Matthew 25:14-30).

Jesus' parable of the talents has traditionally been interpreted as promoting full use and creative enlargement of all the gifts and natural talents God has given to us. Consequently, as we hear in the parable, the two "good and trust-worthy" slaves (vv. 21, 23) who invested and doubled the money that had been given them were complimented and con-gratulated by the master upon his return from his journey. Only the third slave, a "wicked and lazy slave" (v. 26) who dug a hole and hid his master's money, was rebuked and thrown into the outer darkness.

However, another interpretation of this same parable shows the results of ongoing discernment. This second interpretation is based upon the third slave's knowledge that his master was "a harsh man, reaping where [he] did not sow, and gathering where [he] did not scatter seed" (v. 24)—a charge, interestingly enough, that the master himself does not dispute (see v. 26). Furthermore, the first two "good and trustworthy" slaves, along with their master, clearly have taken advantage of others for their own personal gain. These three characters in the parable represent contemporary individuals and corporations that reap where they do not sow and gather where they do not scatter seed—namely, those that prey upon the elderly and the disad-vantaged through outright lies and illegal practices such as pyramid or Ponzi schemes to enlarge their own personal wealth and influence. It is the third slave, the so-called wicked and lazy slave, who clearly stands against those who take advantage of others, who refuses to participate in illegal activities and who short-circuits the ego's obsessions with self-gratification and self-preservation by standing his ground and digging a hole. In this interpretation of the parable, the third slave is the coworker for the kingdom and the ambassador for Christ.

Daily, consistent prayer is the background music for ongo-ing discernment. It helps us to become prayerful, that is, aware and attentive to what God is calling us to do or not do in the present moment.

SPIRITUAL DIRECTION

Spiritual direction is the second spiritual practice of ongoing discernment. It offers an arena where we can share our thoughts, challenges and insights mined from a prayerful assessment of the present situation and from asking, What would Jesus do and how would he do it? This holy conversation with a trusted spiritual companion can be a wonderful aid in naming, claiming and committing to a selfless response to God's call in the present moment.

Every six weeks, Victor meets with his spiritual director. He discusses his work at the law office and his personal life with his family. He talks about how he is seeing God and hearing God's call in the midst of his joys and struggles; he also shares what he hears and learns in prayer, at church and in conversation with others. Rarely, if ever, does he ask specifically for "direction" since he knows only he can live his own life and that his is a unique path to holiness. However, sometimes he'll ask for help and clarification—"Do you have any suggestions about where I can direct my awareness and attention in this situation?"—as he struggles to hear and respond to God's call spoken in his own personal life experience. In discussing his life from the perspective of his commitment to Jesus, Victor is growing in the spirit of prayerful awareness to God's call in his life.

TRUSTFUL SURRENDER

Ongoing discernment requires loving acceptance and trustful surrender to whatever happens at each moment. This third practice is probably the most difficult and misunderstood of all the practices required by ongoing discernment.

The ego, with its self-promoting agenda, protests that such an acceptance and surrender translates into passive resignation to the woes and miseries of life and offers a field day for the devil. It insists upon controlling and manipulating the present moment into a circumstance that it finds more agreeable and less stressful. Furthermore, the ego insists that the kingdom of God just doesn't plop out of nowhere upon us and asserts that the lordship of Jesus Christ must be actively promoted in every situation in which Christians find themselves.

There is certainly no denying the fact that the kingdom of God does not simply materialize out of nowhere without the cooperation of human free will. It is also absolutely true that Christians must actively advance God's will of the lordship of Jesus Christ by the decisions and actions of their lives. Christians are definitely coworkers for the kingdom and ambassadors for Christ.

However, there are times in our lives which seemingly call for the ultimate self-sacrifice, times which we can neither change nor avoid. The written Chinese character for "endurance," "patience" or "persistence" speaks vividly of such situations. It consists of two pictograms. The top pictogram is the Chinese word for "knife." The bottom pictogram is the Chinese word for "heart." Situations which put "a knife in our heart" call for endurance, patience and persistence.

The Christian expression of this Chinese virtue is loving acceptance and trustful surrender. In some situations, this is exactly what selfless openness to this sacred moment means. Far from passive resignation, it is an active response to the present situation rooted in the belief that "all things work together for good for those who love God" (Romans 8:28).

Furthermore, situations which feel like "knives in the heart" are sometimes experienced as a form of discipline (see Hebrews 12:7-11). Our selfless openness to them helps to wean us off the ego's attachment to self-concern, self-image, self-gratification and self-preservation. In this way, what we experience as obstacles can, by God's grace, become aids to our spiritual growth and holiness. As Jesus said, "Every branch that bears fruit [my Father] prunes to make it bear more fruit" (John 15:2).

The belief that God calls us in our human experience is the motivation behind selfless openness to the required duty or unmet need of this sacred moment. This belief breeds the need for awareness of and attention to the present moment, which is the goal of ongoing discernment. Scriptural prayer as well as praying over an experience, commonly called the examen, can also be helpful in supporting the practices of ongoing discernment.

REFLECTION QUESTIONS

1. When has God called you not to take action? How did you discern that?

2. What has been your experience with spiritual direction?

3. When was the last time you were challenged to lovingly accept and trustfully surrender to an experience in life? What doubts and misgivings arose in your heart?

9

DISCOVERING OUR STORY
IN SCRIPTURE

A number of years ago, a friend confided to me that she has a box which contains all the cards and letters her husband had given or sent to her since they had begun to date some twenty-five years ago. Every two years or so, she said, she pulls the box out. She and her husband then go through the cards and letters, reminiscing about their shared history with its joys and struggles. "That box not only carries the history of how my husband and I got to where we are now," she told me, "but it sometimes reminds me how to respond to him."

Scripture is like that box of love letters. Through daily study of it, we come to an understanding of who we are before God and, more importantly, who God calls us to be. We learn our story: the decisions and actions which have blossomed into this sacred moment. We also learn our potential: the reconciliation with all creation under the lordship of Jesus Christ that happens when we respond to the present moment with selfless openness and self-emptying.

Scripture shapes our desires and decisions and teaches us how to respond to this sacred moment as coworkers for the kingdom and ambassadors for Christ. Like old love letters from a spouse, it shows how our ancestors in the faith responded to covenantal duties and obligations. With a contemporary ring, Scripture narrates the prophets' continual challenges to the people of God to turn away from false gods, have a change of heart, and care for the widow, the orphan and the marginalized. It highlights the narrow gate of holiness through which we are called to walk as we follow Jesus' selfless openness and self-emptying, his instructions for life in the Beatitudes, the greatest commandment, and the uncompromising call to forgive and love the enemy. Scripture also gives practical family advice as it enshrines the early church's distillation of Jesus' teaching for emerging communities committed to being of one mind and heart.

Like any other love letter, Scripture is meant to be read with the heart. That's the very essence of scriptural prayer. Scriptural prayer frees the Word of God from any kind of intellectual study in the mind and lets it get beneath the skin and into the heart. It is within the heart that the Word of God then roams, searching for the ball and chain of the ego's agenda. Once we're freed from the shackles of the ego, we can then put flesh and bones on that very Word by the way we respond to this sacred moment. "[W]elcome with meekness the implanted word that has the power to save your souls," James wrote, "but be doers of the word, and not merely hearers who deceive themselves" (1:21-22).

Two traditional forms of spiritual prayer, *lectio divina* and imaginative prayer, are helpful in shaping the attitudes and behaviors which we bring to this sacred moment. They are also helpful in sensitizing us to the call of God and in answering the questions of ongoing discernment, What would Jesus do, and how would he do it?

LECTIO DIVINA

The practice of *lectio divina,* or sacred reading, has its roots in the monastic tradition. However, it continues to be a popular spiritual practice with ordinary Christians committed to responding to this sacred moment. It can be practiced alone or in a communal setting by a family or intentional group.

Individual *lectio divina.*

1. Decide how long you will spend in *lectio divina.* Twenty to thirty minutes is a wise option. The practice of *lectio divina* is done by length of time, not by the length of the chosen Scripture passage.

2. Select a Scripture passage. This can be an event in a Gospel such as a healing, a confrontation or a part of one of the discourses of Jesus. Or it can be a paragraph or short section from one of the New Testament letters. Some of the stories found in Genesis and Exodus as well as the exhortations of the prophets and the Song of Solomon also lend themselves to *lectio divina.* The selection can be made at random, but *lectio divina* works best based on a continued reading of one book at a time. It's important, too, not to bite off more than you can chew; in other words, keep it to a manageable length of about seven to ten verses unless it makes sense to continue with a few more verses. Many translations of the Bible have headings that divide the text for the reader.

3. Start by saying a short prayer to the Holy Spirit asking for the grace to be truly attentive and open to the message that God has waiting for you in this particular scriptural text. This prayer can be augmented with the ritual of tracing a cross over your heart.

4. Read the text slowly and meditatively. Be attentive to it and make sure you intellectually understand the story line or the message that is being conveyed. Reading any editorial notes can be helpful in contextualizing and understanding the event or message.

5. After the first reading of the text, simply sit with the text and notice your reaction to the event or message. How does it move you? Does it remind you of another scriptural event or message, or some event or person in your own life? How and why is the text *personally* addressed to you?

6. Read the text a second time. This time, read it deliberately: word by word, phrase by phrase, verse by verse. Verbalizing it in an audible way can sometimes be helpful. When a word or phrase or verse "jumps off the page" at you or moves you, then stop. Sit with that word, phrase or verse. Roll it around in your mouth like a sip of good wine. "Chew" on it by reflecting on it. Let it interact with you, your behaviors and your attitudes. Let it challenge, mold or enlarge your heart. Don't continue with your reading until you have completely digested this word, phrase or verse.

7. Once you have completely "milked" the word, phrase or verse for all that it has to offer you in this particular sitting, then offer a prayer. You have not authentically encountered Scripture unless you are moved to prayer—a prayer of intercession for a person who comes to mind as you ponder the word, phrase or verse; a prayer of gratitude for a grace received in this sitting of sacred reading; a prayer for forgiveness as you are challenged or convicted by the Word of God; a prayer of praise for the generosity of God exhibited in this word, phrase or verse.

8. Sit in silence for a while after your prayer. This is the time of *lectio divina*'s "afterglow." After about one minute, if a distraction starts to arise, continue with your deliberate reading of the Scripture passage until another word, phrase or verse "jumps off the page" at you or moves you. Then repeat steps six, seven and eight. The purpose of *lectio divina* is not to "get through" the selected scriptural passage; it is to be transformed by the Word of God.

9. Before your time comes to an end, commit a word, phrase or verse from the selected Scripture passage to memory. This can serve as a "mantra" which you can repeat periodically throughout the day to call to mind the grace of this sitting. It might also serve as a reminder for the way you want to live your life.

10. Conclude your period of *lectio divina* with a prayer to God. Thank the Father for the gift of the saving Word in your life. Praise the Father for the gift of Jesus, the Word made flesh in your life and the source of your salvation. Petition the Holy Spirit to give you the insight, courage and determination to give birth to the Word of God by the way you live your life.

Group *lectio divina*.

1. After your group gathers together, the chosen leader begins by offering a vocal prayer to the Holy Spirit that each member of the group be attentive and open to the grace that God wishes to bestow upon your group and its members in this practice of *lectio divina*. This prayer is followed by a short period of silence.

2. The leader slowly and meditatively reads the selected

Scripture passage. The passage could be the New Testament reading or Gospel reading for the upcoming Sunday from the common lectionary. Or it could be a Scripture passage around which your group feels some "energy."

3. After the slow and meditative reading of the passage, each member silently ponders the passage for one to two minutes.

4. The leader slowly and meditatively reads the passage a second time.

5. After the second reading and thirty seconds of silence, each member is invited to simply repeat aloud the word, phrase or verse that "moved" or "spoke to" them. No commentary is offered.

6. Once the members have each individually shared their word, phrase or verse, the Scripture passage is read for a third time.

7. After the third reading and thirty seconds of silence, each member is invited to share why the particular word, phrase or verse mentioned in step five is meaningful, challenging or comforting to them.

8. Once all the members have shared their commentary, a period of silence follows. Then members are free to share any spontaneous vocal prayer they might be moved to pray.

9. The leader ends the group *lectio divina* with a concluding spontaneous prayer. This can be followed by a communal recitation of the Lord's Prayer.

IMAGINATIVE PRAYER
Imaginative prayer has a five-hundred-year history as a practice of spiritual formation. Using a Gospel scene, it engages both

the imagination and the emotions.

1. Unlike *lectio divina,* which has a predetermined time limit, imaginative prayer has an open-ended time limit. It is best done when you can enter deeply into the Gospel story without concern for the amount of time you are spending with the passage. Time constraints put pressure on you and can be a hindrance to imaginative prayer.

2. Select a scene or incident from the life of Jesus from one of the Gospels.

3. Start by saying a short prayer to the Holy Spirit asking for the grace to be truly attentive and open to the message that God has waiting for you in this particular Gospel scene. This prayer can be augmented with the ritual of tracing a cross over your heart.

4. Read the passage slowly and meditatively about three or four times. Get a sense of the scene's flow and chain of events. Note each of the characters, including Jesus, and how they respond to what is going on.

5. Now place yourself in the scene. For example, if you are praying over the story of the woman caught in adultery (see John 8:1-11), picture yourself in the crowd as the scribes and Pharisees bring the woman before Jesus. What are you thinking? What are you feeling? Do you identify with the self-righteousness of the scribes and Pharisees? Do you feel compassion for the woman caught in adultery? Why or why not? What do you think Jesus is writing on the ground? Ponder your reactions for insights into yourself, your past, your attitudes and your behaviors.

6. Now picture yourself as one of the scribes or Pharisees.

What emotional need does it satisfy inside of you to bring this public sinner to Jesus? When have you publicized someone else's sin in conversation or gossip? How do you intellectually and emotionally respond to Jesus' statement "Let anyone among you who is without sin be the first to throw a stone at her"? How long does it take you to slip away? Ponder your reactions for insights into yourself, your past, your attitudes and your behaviors.

7. Now place yourself in the role of the woman caught in adultery. Do you have trouble relating to her? What is going on within your heart as you and your sin are publicly paraded in front of everyone? What is your feeling toward the scribes and Pharisees who bring you to Jesus? When has a sin of yours been made public against your will? How did you respond? What happens inside of you as you hear Jesus say, "Neither do I condemn you. Go your way, and from now on do not sin again"? Ponder your reactions for insights into yourself, your past, your attitudes and your behaviors.

8. Now place yourself in the role of Jesus. What is your reaction to the scribes and Pharisees? How do you look upon the woman caught in adultery? What are you writing on the ground? Why do you choose not to condemn such a terrible sinner? Ponder your reactions for insights into yourself, your past, your attitudes and your behaviors.

9. Once you have thoroughly explored the Gospel scene and placed yourself in the shoes of all the characters, make a deliberate and informed resolution to change an attitude or behavior in light of your experience of the Gospel passage. Let this resolution become your mission until the next time you imaginatively pray over the life of Jesus.

10. Conclude your period of imaginative prayer with a prayer to God. Thank the Father for the gift of the saving Word in your life. Praise the Father for the gift of Jesus, the Word made flesh in your life and the source of your salvation. Petition the Holy Spirit to give you the insight, courage and determination to give birth to the Word of God by being faithful to your resolution.

Virginia, now in her seventies, looked forward to retirement from her job as the church secretary. She told me once that she has spent a part of every day since her retirement praying with Scripture, sometimes using *lectio divina,* sometimes using imaginative prayer. I still remember when she came for spiritual direction and sat down, grinning from ear to ear. When I asked the cause of her joy, she simply replied, "There are days when the words of Scripture stretch me in ways I never thought—and tickle me to death!" As she proceeded to tell me how her prayer over Jesus' ministry to the sick has led her to volunteer at a residence for Alzheimer's patients, I was reminded of the transformative power of the Word of God and James's exhortation to "be doers of the word" (James 1:22). Scripture has become Virginia's story—and it has the potential to become ours as we immerse ourselves in it and use it to foster ongoing discernment.

REFLECTION QUESTIONS

1. What has been your experience with *lectio divina* and imaginative prayer? What attitudes and behaviors have they instilled in your life?

2. When was the last time a Scripture passage "jumped off the page" at you, moved you or convicted you? What was the passage? What thoughts and emotions arose inside of you?

3. How does the Word of God inform the words of your lips? How does the Word of God inform your daily actions and decisions?

IO

~

DEVELOPING A
REFLECTIVE LIFESTYLE

*F*or a very long time, people would only have to spend about one hour with me before experiencing one of my greatest shortcomings: I was impatient and had a short fuse. At the drop of a hat, I could go bananas, hit the roof, fly off the handle, and have a conniption fit over the slightest little inconvenience or irritation. My weakness used to be a target of kidding and teasing by many; it was also a source of worry and concern for me. Typical of a classic Type A personality, I habitually reacted without pausing, pondering and reflecting.

Over the years, every spiritual director I had challenged and encouraged me to develop a reflective lifestyle—an unhurried way of living that short-circuits spur-of-the-moment emotional outbursts or reactions. A reflective lifestyle incorporates meditative behaviors and contemplative habits that lead to informed and thoughtful responses; it also values time spent reviewing what's going on in daily life and reflecting on what the five senses are experiencing, knowing such practices foster sensi-

tivity to the variety of ways in which God calls us. Characterized by a daily spirit of recollection, a reflective lifestyle is not
about primping in the mirror, navel-gazing or self-absorption;
it is about looking out the window and cultivating selfless
openness to this sacred moment. The authentic fruit of such a
lifestyle is the emptying of self for the enrichment of others.

Many years ago I was introduced to a spiritual practice that
has helped me develop a reflective lifestyle. The richness of this
practice lies in its fruit that spills over into a person's ordinary
and waking consciousness: a patient, attentive and spontaneous response to the present moment. Though I still struggle
with my Type A personality, I now typically catch myself and
stop any instant knee-jerk emotional action. I'm learning to
pause, ponder and respond as a result of this daily and consistent spiritual practice.

The practice is called the examen. It has a five-hundred-year
history and is based upon the belief that God calls in the ordinary experiences of daily life. Usually done at lunchtime and in
the evening before going to bed, it takes about fifteen minutes.
The examen invites us to revisit the past hours of the day and,
sensitive to the thoughts and feelings we experienced, ask
where, how and why God was calling in the required duty or
unmet need of a particular moment.

Traditionally the examen has five steps: gratitude (reviewing
God's gifts during the day with the gratitude that arises from
such awareness), petition (praying for the grace of understanding and insight into God's call so we may respond to the divine
invitation), review (surveying the events of the day and noting
God's call to be a coworker for the kingdom and how we responded), forgiveness (expressing sorrow and asking forgiveness for our deliberate deafness and lack of response to God's
call) and renewal (anticipating the events of the following day

and how we will respond to God's call to continued growth). Amazingly, this fifteen-minute practice fosters a spirit of ongoing discernment.

THE INDIVIDUAL EXAMEN

The five steps are not fixed and definitive. Flexibility is allowed depending on our personalities and the experience of our day. As a matter of fact, sometimes the practice of the examen will focus on just one or two of the steps. The challenge of the practice is daily and consistent fidelity to it, not getting through each individual step each time we practice it.

Here's a typical way to get started with this spiritual practice:

1. Say a short prayer to the Holy Spirit asking for the grace to be truly attentive and open to the call that God had waiting for you in the past few hours.

2. Adopt a reflective, recollective mood and objectively overview the most recent hours that have passed. Note any event, circumstance or incident that evoked feelings of praise and gratitude to God. Render thanks and praise to God for such experiences. Don't be too quick to move on to the next step; wait until you feel fully satisfied with this step.

3. Note any event, circumstance or incident that evoked a strong emotional response from you. The response could be either positive or negative. Don't attribute blame, criticism or anger to yourself or another; just observe in a neutral way the incident and your reaction.

4. As you observe your reaction, ask if this incident or ones like it are typical in your life. Do your reaction and response remain the same in such situations or did they change this time? If they changed, why? What image comes to mind that

helps you make sense of this experience? Is there a Gospel scene that is analogous to this situation? Thoroughly analyze the situation and your response as much as you can. Again, don't be too quick to move on to the next step; wait until you feel fully satisfied with this step.

5. Now move from the mood of self-reflection to a mood of selfless openness. What was God's call in the duty or need of that event, circumstance or incident? What specifically was God saying to you in that situation? Were you aware of it at the time or are you only coming to hear God's call now as you remember and reflect upon the experience?

6. Take the call of God in this experience and express it in a simple statement. This sentence can serve as both a challenge and a reminder of God's presence when you find yourself in a similar situation. Writing it down and later comparing it with other statements from the past can be an excellent way to get in touch with and become sensitive to the way God specifically speaks to you. You'll soon discover key themes that run throughout God's love relationship with you.

7. Express your sorrow to God for your insensitivity or lack of willingness to respond to his numerous calls to you in the past few hours of the day.

8. Take a few moments and anticipate the upcoming hours or tomorrow. Where might you need to be diligently attentive to the sacred moment? How might God surprise you with a call in the required duty or unmet need that stands before you?

9. Conclude with a prayer of praise and thanksgiving to God

for the manifold ways God calls you to holiness through a selfless openness and self-emptying in this and every sacred moment.

The results of the examen can provide an excellent subject for a spiritual direction session.

THE FAMILY EXAMEN

The examen can also be practiced in a family setting, a community setting or any setting where a group of people gathers intentionally for a specific purpose. A church staff, as it plans for its individual church's future, might find it helpful in deepening awareness to how God might be calling the entire church congregation.

Here's a typical way to get started with this spiritual practice in a group setting:

1. The family or intentional group gathers together to remember and reflect upon a specific incident from the past or its communal history. The past incident could be a joyful occasion such as a family reunion or a time of grief such as burying a loved one. It could also be an experience that requires discernment such as a planning meeting for the future, a transfer to another city, the choice of a new pastor, or the appropriate response to an unmet need in the family or community. Any shared experience is appropriate.

   Unlike the individual examen, which usually takes about fifteen minutes, the family or communal experience of the examen can require as much as one hour. It should not be rushed, and each member should be able to speak freely.

2. Start by saying a short prayer to the Holy Spirit asking for the grace to be truly attentive and open to God's call in this shared experience.

3. As a group, adopt a reflective, recollective mood and objectively overview the shared experience or event, noting the reasons for praise and gratitude to God. Share those reasons verbally and include a prayer of thanks and praise to God.

4. Each member of the family or group shares his or her experience of the event. This includes what they were thinking and feeling and why they might have responded the way they did. Blame, criticism or anger toward oneself or toward another is inappropriate and should be avoided.

5. After each member has shared his or her thoughts, feelings and reactions to the experience, ponder the following questions together: What was God calling us to as a family or group in the moment this event happened? Is there an image or Gospel scene that comes to mind that helps your family or group hear the call of God spoken in this event? Members are allowed to share their thoughts and feelings.

6. The members now move to an explicit stance of selfless openness. What is God's call right now in the circumstances that are a result of this event or incident? What specifically is God saying to your family or group in this resulting situation? Each member shares his or her thoughts or feelings.

7. Take the call of God in this shared experience and express it in a simple statement. This sentence can serve as both a challenge and a reminder of God's presence with your family or group. Writing it down and later comparing it with other statements from the past can be an excellent way to get in touch with and become sensitive to the way that God

specifically speaks to your family or group. You'll soon discover key themes that run throughout God's love relationship with your family or group.

8. Don't worry or be concerned if your family or group members cannot reach an agreement about what God is saying in a particular event or circumstance. Praying as a family or group over a shared experience a second or third time can sometimes prove helpful. But some insights into God's call can take a long time to be discovered, unearthed and understood. Also, some insights are meant to be more personal than communal.

9. As a family or group, express your sorrow to God for your insensitivity or lack of willingness to respond to God's numerous calls.

10. Conclude with a prayer of praise and thanksgiving to God for the manifold ways God calls your family or group to holiness through a selfless openness and self-emptying in this and every sacred moment. Include with it the family's or group's continued desire to work for God's kingdom in the world and for the reconciliation of all creation under the lordship of Jesus Christ.

No other spiritual practice has affected me as powerfully and profoundly as the examen, practiced individually and communally. The individual examen has led me at times to be spontaneously aware of God's presence and call in this sacred moment even before I reflect upon this moment later in the day. Practicing the examen in a community setting continues to remind me that God intentionally calls us not just as individuals but also as a family to be coworkers for the kingdom and ambassadors for Christ.

REFLECTION QUESTIONS

1. What practices do you use to help promote a reflective, recollected lifestyle?

2. How can the daily practice of the examen help you grow in selfless openness to this sacred moment? How can you fit it into your daily schedule?

3. Has your family recently experienced a shared event that would lend itself to a family examen? How might family members hear a different call from God in it than you do?

THE OBSTACLE OF THE EGO

*A*rthur and Caroline, along with two other couples whom they had known for over twenty-five years, had just finished an anniversary meal in a fine restaurant. As the six of them were walking out of the restaurant and heading for a stroll along the lake, a beggar approached, asking for a handout. Arthur wanted to give, but, sensing the displeasure of his friends toward the beggar, he didn't. As they walked along, his wife and the other couples complained about the abundance of panhandlers in the city and how they can be such a nuisance. Arthur was tempted to speak up and disagree but feared how his wife and friends might react. And so, for the sake of his reputation, he kept silent.

The ego—with its consuming passion and preoccupation with what we have, what we do and what people think of us—is the primary deterrent to selfless openness to this sacred moment. Its very nature is to be self-absorbed, to primp in front of the mirror, and to evaluate any decision or action in light of its two major objectives: survival and self-aggrandizement. These two objectives find their practical expression in the ego's obsession with self-concern, self-image, self-gratification and self-preservation.

SELF-CONCERN

Self-concern is one way that the ego manages to obstruct a selfless response to this sacred moment. When I'm self-concerned, I become totally focused on myself and my own interests; before responding to God's call in the moment, I ask myself, *What's in it for me?* And if I do not come up with a satisfactory answer, I hesitate to respond or decide not to respond at all.

Just about everyone who meets Martha walks away thinking she is one of the most selfish and self-centered people they will ever meet. Behind her back, people refer to her as "Me-Me" because seemingly every sentence out of her mouth begins with "I" or is referenced to herself. She counsels anyone who listens to "look out for Number One" and certainly follows that advice. Her natural and immediate inclination is to think of herself before others. This attitude and behavior blinds her to the needs of others and makes her deaf to God's call to be compassionate or charitable.

Though Martha is a rare example of self-concern in the extreme, she reminds us that self-absorption can lead to a fixation with the self where we constantly reach out not to enrich the lives of others but to grab for ourselves. We become content to worship at a side altar filled with mirrors.

SELF-IMAGE

An excessive investment in one's *self-image* can also hinder us from responding to the sacred moment. This investment is betrayed by an overconcern for or fear of what others might think. It's what Arthur struggled with that night after dinner when the beggar approached. It could also be why Nicodemus, perhaps a member of the Sanhedrin and thus a very public Jewish leader, decided to visit Jesus "by night" instead of during the day (see John 3:1-21).

In addition, a fixation on self-image causes us to get caught in the trap of comparing ourselves with other people. Rather than responding to the duty or need of this sacred moment in which we find ourselves, we are always trying to manufacture what is thought to be a "holier" scenario or to duplicate someone else's path of holiness.

I have always said that being a Franciscan is part of my DNA. Even with my Jesuit education, I have always had a natural inclination toward and attraction to the Franciscan vision and approach to life. However, after professing temporary vows as a Franciscan, I went through a period of disillusionment. I still remember the day I saw my spiritual director and said to him, "You know, I don't think I am meant to be a Franciscan."

My spiritual director raised an eyebrow in surprise. "What on earth are you talking about?" he asked.

I replied, "Well, Saint Francis used to take a walk in the woods and would immediately get caught up in the presence of God. I, on the other hand, take a walk in the woods and usually come back with bird droppings on my shoulders or poison ivy. I just can't find God the way Saint Francis did."

My spiritual director gave me some wise counsel. "I don't think God is asking you to become another Francis of Assisi. God already has one. I think what would give God the most pleasure and delight is if you became the best Albert Haase that God created you to be. That's the real secret to spiritual formation and contemporary holiness."

Now, after living as a Franciscan friar for more than thirty years, I understand the wisdom of that spiritual director. Rather than trying to rigidly duplicate someone else's path to holiness, whether it be that of Francis of Assisi or Dietrich Bonhoeffer or Mother Teresa of Calcutta, the real challenge is to selflessly respond to God's call in the sacred moment in which I find myself. That is, in effect, what all the great saints have done. And that is how the path to holiness is paved for each one of us.

A preoccupation with self-image is also betrayed when we find ourselves fussing over the fear of failure. I still remember the day when, having returned to the United States after almost twelve years as a missionary in mainland China, I was asked to join the theology faculty at Quincy University. Even though I was initially excited about the idea, I was at the same time also riddled with fear. *What if I don't have the knack for teaching?* I thought. *What if I am a dud when it comes to relating with college students? What will the friars say if I am not successful?* I fretted about those fears for months before I finally headed to Quincy. Fear can paralyze our selfless and immediate response to this sacred moment.

We are wrapped up in our self-image when we have an emotional need to "look" holy. This can be as blatant as being overly sensitive to what people might be thinking or whispering as we walk into a church, or it can be as subtle as a pharisaical spirituality that canonizes the external and is merely skin-deep. When we are obsessed with the trappings of holiness for the sake of appearances, we can easily miss out on God's call in this sacred moment. Always primping in the mirror, we become blind and deaf to the beggar's outstretched hand, the cries for justice and peace, and the requests for compassion by those who stand right in front of us.

SELF-GRATIFICATION

The ego obstructs selfless openness with an emotional investment in *self-gratification*. This is inherently focused on my desires and best interests. Sometimes it is played out in an indulgent lifestyle that lacks self-control and is fixated upon pleasure, power and possessions.

Self-gratification is the polar opposite of self-emptying for the enrichment of others. Luke illustrates this in chapter 9 of his Gospel. A would-be disciple who had an emotional need for comfort fell by the wayside when Jesus reminded him of the consequences of selfless openness to the present moment: "Foxes have holes, and birds of the air have nests; but the Son of Man has nowhere to lay his head" (v. 58). Jesus also showed two other potential disciples that the immediate and selfless response to God's call precludes even the pleasure and personal fulfillment that comes from performing the appropriate action or filial obligation such as saying farewell or burying one's parent (see vv. 59-62).

The required duty or unmet need of this sacred moment sometimes challenges us to take a step in faith immediately and at great risk. It brooks no competition and often does not wait for us to work things out to our personal advantage or according to our convenience. The ego's fixation upon self-gratification, sometimes expressed as a need to have our "ducks in a row," can thus delay or altogether hinder a selfless response to God's call. And that delay can be the deal breaker for this transforming moment of grace. Indeed, timing is everything when it comes to God's call expressed in this sacred moment.

According to the first three Gospels, some of the disciples responded with a selfless openness to Jesus' invitation that we can only describe as a radical step in faith. At the time of Jesus, the Jewish custom was for students to approach rabbis and ask to become their disciples. This is how John's Gospel portrays disciples leaving John the Baptist for Jesus (see John 1:35-42) and was probably what happened in the case of Paul studying under Gamaliel (see Acts 22:3). The first three Gospels, however, have a different interpretation of what happened. They record Jesus inviting people to follow him (see Matthew 4:18-22; Mark 2:13-17; Luke 5:1-11, 27-32). In one case, the Gospel of Luke says the disciples left everything "immediately"; the implication in the other cases is, similarly, that they responded on the spot: "When they had brought their boats to shore, they left everything and followed him" (Luke 5:11). A selfless response to this sacred moment sometimes requires an immediacy which forfeits the security and self-gratification that the ego demands.

SELF-PRESERVATION

The ego's final obstacle to selfless openness is its obsession with *self-preservation*. Mortally afraid of losing control and of moving beyond its comfort zone, the ego thrives on and strives for safety and security. And yet, God's call in this sacred moment often moves us beyond what is comfortable, pleasant and easy. As a matter of fact, a challenging or apparently impossible call is a pretty good sign that something larger than the ego is at work. A spiritual directee of mine, referring to Jesus' invitation to Peter to get out of the boat and walk on water (see Matthew 14:22-33), hit the nail on the head when he said, "We have a choice of being either deck-huggers or wave-walkers. Most of us never experience the meaning of faith because *we're still in the boat!*"

We see how an emotional fixation on self-preservation can be a barrier to selfless openness to God's call in the story of the rich man (see Mark 10:17-22). The man was undoubtedly a religious person since he had kept the commandments. With love, Jesus offered him an invitation: "Go, sell what you own, and give the money to the poor, and you will have treasure in heaven; then come, follow me" (v. 21). The ego's tightening grip around the rich man's heart is betrayed in the following verse: "When he heard this, he was shocked and went away grieving, for he had many possessions" (v. 22). Self-preservation became the insurmountable hurdle blocking the rich man's selfless response to the call of the moment. He was possessed by his own possessions.

The ego promotes dogged self-centeredness and uncompromising individuality—a life obsessed with self-concern, self-image, self-gratification and self-preservation. At its worst, it leads far away from selfless openness to this sacred moment and devolves into a self-absorbed, self-loving, narcissistic and hedonistic lifestyle.

Thankfully, Jesus shows us the path to freedom from the ego and to holiness right here, right now.

REFLECTION QUESTIONS

1. How do you know when an emotional attachment to self-concern, self-image, self-gratification or self-preservation is hindering you from responding to God's call? What are the characteristics of this attachment?

2. When has the fear of failure stopped you from responding to God's call? What spiritual practices can help you overcome such fear?

3. Would you characterize yourself as a deck-hugger or a wave-walker? Why?

12

THE GOSPEL'S ANTIDOTE

*F*rancis of Assisi is one of the most well-known and beloved saints of all time. He is popularly known for preaching to the birds and for his love for all creation. He's also known for his radical lifestyle of poverty and humility. However, probably only the scholar is aware of Francis's unique contribution to the history of Christian spirituality.

All the established religious orders at Francis's time, such as those that followed the Rule of Life written by Saint Augustine or Saint Benedict, looked to the early Christians as described in the Acts of the Apostles for justification of their lifestyle and for inspiration about how to live. Specifically, they looked to the description found in chapter four, which highlights the importance of community life and the communal sharing of goods: "Now the whole group of those who believed were of one heart and soul, and no one claimed private ownership of any possessions, but everything they owned was held in common" (Acts 4:32).

Francis of Assisi, however, chose a different emphasis for his life. Rather than look to the early Christian community's interpretation of the ideals of Christ for inspiration, Francis went straight back to the life of Jesus as described in the Gospels as the explicit and definitive benchmark for his lifestyle and for those who wished to follow in his footsteps. The Rule he wrote, approved by Pope Honorius III in 1223, begins with a simple expression that bears a weighty challenge: "The Rule and Life of the Lesser Brothers is this: to observe the Holy Gospel of Our Lord Jesus Christ." And throughout his life, he continually insisted that those who follow him live the Gospels strictly and literally, without interpretation and without gloss.

Francis of Assisi's use of the Gospels rather than the Acts of the Apostles as his guide for how to live reveals a keen insight: living according to the gospel illumines the path to freedom from the ego and to a holiness that is timeless.

IMITATION OF CHRIST

The teachings of Jesus come into direct opposition and clash with the self-centered agenda of the ego. Peter's experience is a case in point. At Caesarea Philippi, Peter's image in front of the other disciples shines as he is the first disciple to proclaim Jesus as the Messiah (see Mark 8:27-30). However, as soon as Jesus expresses his understanding of being a Messiah who will be rejected and killed, Peter pulls him aside and refuses to accept the reality of Jesus' words. After all, such an understanding is devastating to a life based upon the ego. Jesus rebukes Peter, calling him a satan for focusing his mind "not on divine things but on human things" (Mark 8:33), and then teaches that egotistical self-aggrandizement and the obsession with self-preservation are not the path to holiness; rather, the path to holiness is paved with self-emptying for the sake of others:

> If any want to become my followers, let them deny themselves and take up their cross and follow me. For those

who want to save their life will lose it, and those who lose their life for my sake, and for the sake of the gospel, will save it. For what will it profit them to gain the whole world and forfeit their life? Indeed, what can they give in return for their life? (Mark 8:34-37).

At the heart of Jesus' teaching is denying and losing one's life—self-emptying for the sake of others. This is what it means to take up the cross. This is the essence of imitating Christ. In a paradox that thousands of believers in history have discovered as true, loss and emptying of self leads to a fulfillment that is experienced as salvation. And indeed it is a kind of salvation, for the one who loses their life is rescued from the constricting clutches of the ego.

Mother Teresa of Calcutta and her Missionaries of Charity immediately come to mind as perfect examples. As their spiritual director in Asia for a number of years, I came to know the sisters and their lifestyle very well. In all my life as a priest, I have never met women so committed to a life of radical selflessness for the sake of others. Their name, Missionaries of Charity, says it all. Being with the sisters, you immediately experience the joy and happiness that come with a life focused on compassion, kindness and concern for others. Their imitation of Christ frees them from the selfishness of the ego.

Jesus reiterated his teaching on denying ourselves and made it even more explicit when he suspected his disciples were arguing about which one of them was the greatest. Holiness, he explained, is about being selflessly open to God's call in this sacred moment: "Whoever wants to be first must be last of all and servant of all" (Mark 9:35). It is about attending to and serving the duty or needs of the present moment. He later explicitly highlighted the fact that holiness is becoming a "slave" for the enrichment of others: "Whoever wishes to become great among you must be your servant, and whoever wishes to be first among you must be [the] slave of all. For the Son of Man came not to be served but to serve, and to give his life a ransom for many" (Mark 10:43-45). Such a teaching flies in the face of the ego's preoccupation and infatuation with self-concern, self-image, self-gratification and self-preservation.

Jesus then placed a child in the midst of his disciples and, embracing the child, said, "Whoever welcomes one such child in my name welcomes me, and whoever welcomes me welcomes not me but the one who sent me" (Mark 9:37). This was clearly a countercultural gesture. In Jesus' day, due to the high mortality rate, children were considered invisible until they reached the beginning of adolescence. Jesus not only raised the status of children and acknowledged their presence in this gesture, but also, by his self-identification with them, he challenged the ego's investment in self-image. Furthermore, he noted that selfless openness to an apparently insignificant child is an action rendered on behalf of "the one who sent me." Indeed, any and every moment bears the potential of an encounter with God.

FAITH VERSUS FEAR

Jesus also exposed the ego's use of fear as a ruse that makes us hesitate to respond. Fear of failure, of what others might think, of being unprepared, of our unworthiness or our inability can run the gamut from outright alarm and panic to dismay, distress and anxiety. And fear is insidious because it jolts us out of this sacred moment; we grovel in the past with guilt and regret, or we rush headlong into the future with worry and apprehension.

That's why Jesus was quick to tell us to stay put and selflessly respond to the present moment. He reminded us of the caring providence of God and the uselessness of worry and anxiety (see Matthew 6:25-34), suggesting a contemplative practice of paying attention to and reflecting upon what our five senses are experiencing (vv. 26, 28). He also encouraged us to remain in this sacred moment and proposed faith as the antidote to fear, anxiety and worry: "Indeed your heavenly Father knows that you need all these things. But strive first for the kingdom of God and his righteousness, and all these things will be given to you as well. So do not worry about tomorrow" (vv. 32-34).

When his disciples asked for an "increase" in faith, Jesus taught that it is not a noun, not a quantitative commodity that can be measured or weighed. It is, rather, a verb found in ongoing discernment's practice of trustful surrender to what is before us in this sacred moment: "If you had faith the size of a mustard seed," Jesus said, "you could say to this mulberry tree, 'Be uprooted and planted in the sea,' and it would obey you" (Luke 17:6). Jesus' emphasis on "this mulberry tree" makes it evident that we live our faith in "this" present and sacred moment. Faith overcomes fear and anxiety by *believing* in the impossible now; it is focused on God, not the ego: "What is impossible for mortals is possible for God" (Luke 18:27).

THE IMPORTANCE OF NOW

Jesus' hyperbolic challenge to tear out an eye or cut off the hand (see Matthew 5:29-30) as well as his teaching on the impossibility of serving two masters (see Matthew 6:24) highlight the urgency and immediacy of God's call in this sacred moment. Despite the ego's temptation to postpone a response because of personal inconvenience or family obligations (see Luke 9:57-62), Jesus reminds us that timing is everything and the time is *now*.

Watchful, eager anticipation and faithful readiness for an encounter with God in any and every ordinary moment are the point of Jesus' story in Matthew 25:1-13. In the parable, ten bridesmaids went out to meet the bridegroom. The five wise ones took their lamps with extra flasks of oil, a symbol of ongoing discernment and selfless openness to any and every sacred moment, while the five foolish ones went out with only their lamps, symbolic of a cosmetic spirituality that merely looked prepared. Since the bridegroom delayed, the ten bridesmaids fell asleep as their lamps burned. When the bridegroom suddenly made his appearance unexpectedly at midnight, the foolish bridesmaids were caught unawares and without adequate oil. While they were off purchasing more oil, the wedding banquet was started, the wise bridesmaids entered with the bridegroom and the door was shut. Upon their return, the foolish bridesmaids were unable to enter the banquet. Jesus succinctly summed up the lesson of the parable: "Keep awake therefore, for you know neither the day nor the hour" (Matthew 25:13).

Immediate awareness fostered by the practices of ongoing discernment and selfless openness to a sudden divine encounter in this sacred moment requires the imitation of Christ and freedom from the ego. However, sheer willpower is not enough to attain them. They are possible only through the gift of God's Spirit in our lives.

REFLECTION QUESTIONS

1. Which Gospel story or saying of Jesus is especially challenging or helpful for you in your own spiritual formation? Why?

2. In what ways and in which circumstances do you make a conscious effort to imitate Christ? How is that imitation expressed?

3. What spiritual practices help you to stay prepared and awake for God's call in this sacred moment?

13

THE TRAITS
OF SELFLESSNESS

During a spiritual direction session, Stuart told me how he was finding the practice of *lectio divina* very helpful. "I never knew that meditating on Scripture could be so life-giving and energizing," he said. "And, as a side note," he continued, "I learned something."

"What's that?" I asked.

"For so many years, I have prayed and asked the Holy Spirit to come into my life and to guide me and my decisions. But praying with Scripture has taught me that I don't have to pray *for* the Holy Spirit. I *already have* the Spirit! As a matter of fact, I am a temple of the Holy Spirit. My challenge is to live *in* the Spirit and to keep the fire of the Spirit blazing in my life, as St. Paul says."

I leaned back in my chair and momentarily thought about how Stuart had just hit the nail on the head. The gift of the Spirit comes to us in baptism and abides within us. And yet, we sometimes forget to give full rein to the Spirit and follow the Spirit's lead. A selfless response to God's call in this sacred moment is a reliable indicator that we are living in the Spirit and stoking the Spirit's fire in our lives.

THE GIFT OF THE SPIRIT

The words *spiritual* formation, *spirit*uality and *spirit*ual life all highlight the central and decisive role that the Holy Spirit plays in the life of the Christian. A friend of mine who is a computer specialist rightly calls the Spirit the "operating system" of the believer. Indeed, without "the Lord and Giver of life," as proclaimed in the Nicene Creed, we would spend our days on death row shackled to the walls of the ego's dark and dank prison cell.

But with the risen Christ's gift of the Spirit given "without measure" (see John 3:34; 20:22), the door of that prison cell swings open and the shackles fall to the ground: "where the Spirit of the Lord is, there is freedom" (2 Corinthians 3:17). And that means freedom from the ego. More than a mere reprieve, this gift is the "first installment" of all that God has promised us; it is the "guarantee" of eternal life, the "seal" and "pledge" of our future inheritance as children of God (see 2 Corinthians 1:22; 5:5; Ephesians 1:13-14; 4:30; Romans 8:14). Abiding with us and in us, the Spirit transforms our bodies into temples and sanctifies our lives (see John 14:17; Romans 8:9; 1 Corinthians 6:19; 2 Thessalonians 2:13; 1 Peter 1:2). Paul highlighted this formative and transformative power of the Spirit and the change that takes place through the Holy Spirit when he referred to us as "slaves . . . in the new life of the Spirit" (Romans 7:6) and called one Christian community "a letter of Christ . . . written not with ink but with the Spirit of the living God" (2 Corinthians 3:3).

The gift of the Spirit not only frees us *from* the ego's obsession with self-concern, self-image, self-gratification and self-preservation but also frees us *for* the enrichment of others and the community—"for the common good," as Paul reminded the Corinthians (1 Corinthians 12:7). This is what self-emptying is all about. Using a farming image to describe the consequences of a life according to the ego—what Paul calls "flesh"—and a life according to the Spirit, Paul wrote to the Christian community at Galatia:

> Do not be deceived; God is not mocked, for you reap whatever you sow. If you sow to your own flesh, you will reap corruption from the flesh; but if you sow to the Spirit, you will reap eternal life from the Spirit. So let us not grow weary in doing what is right, for we will reap at harvesttime, if we do not give up. So then, whenever we have an opportunity, let us work for the good of all, and especially for those of the family of faith. (Galatians 6:7-10)

Being selflessly open to the duty or need of this sacred moment—working "for the good of all"—is sowing seed in the new life of the Spirit.

THE FRUIT OF THE SPIRIT

Paul encourages Christians to live in the Spirit, according to the Spirit and guided by the Spirit (see Romans 8:5; Galatians 5:16, 25). Such a lifestyle is characterized by nine traits which he calls "the fruit of the Spirit": "love, joy, peace, patience, kindness, generosity, faithfulness, gentleness, and self-control" (Galatians 5:22-23). Five of the traits—joy, peace, patience, gentleness and self-control—are the fruit of the selflessness that the Spirit calls forth in this sacred moment. I'll discuss these traits in this chapter and the other four traits in the next chapter.

To live in the Spirit is to experience a life of *joy* and *peace*. These two traits of a Spirit-led life should not simply be equated with an exuberance about life and a restful serenity. In many respects, exuberance and serenity are superficial sentiments or feelings. Rather, the Spirit's joy and peace are rooted deep within the heart of the believer and are nourished by the reality of Christ's resurrection, the stunning proclamation that the power of evil has been definitively conquered and that earthly death is the passage to eternal life. This is the preeminent source of the Christian's joy and peace.

John Vianney was a famous priest of the nineteenth century. People from all over Europe traveled to the small French town of Ars to seek his counsel and consolation. Because of his extraordinary holiness, Vianney experienced personal battles with the devil, whom he nicknamed *le Grappin* ("the Claw"), which was a toothed instrument used to grub in a garden. These battles started under cover of night but were soon manifested during the day. A famous incident occurred in 1838 when a young student, Denis Chaland, went to confession in the kitchen of Vianney's presbytery. Halfway through the confession, the whole room started to violently shake. Terrified, Chaland got up off his knees and attempted to flee. However, John Vianney held his arm and prevented him. "It's nothing," Vianney calmly reassured him. "It's *only* the devil!"

That humorous comment calmly spoken during a dramatic demonic attack betrays the Spirit's joy and peace which come with the awareness of "the power of [Christ's] resurrection" (Philippians 3:10). The power of evil has been conquered; death has lost its sting. As one spiritual directee of mine enjoys saying, "Spiritual formation and the spiritual life are certainly experienced in a whole different way when you realize the Super Bowl is over and the final score has entered the history books. We live during the postgame show."

In addition to joy and peace, a Spirit-led selflessness blossoms in a life of *patience*. In one sense, this trait expands our hearts. It gives us the ability and capacity to accept delay or tolerate trouble and suffering without the ego's knee-jerk reaction of anger. This trait engenders trustful surrender to inconvenience.

However, there is another dimension to the Spirit's fruit of patience, and it is expressed in the willingness to persevere, to persist and to stick with things. It is the faithful allegiance that we give to God, our closest friends, and the peace and justice issues which burn within our lives. I see this kind of patience in the spiritual directee who intentionally and deliberately keeps showing up for daily prayer and devotion even though they are currently in the midst of a prolonged "dry period" and spiritual desert. I see it in Teresa's meticulous care and daily concern for her husband, whose life has been flooded by the waves of Alzheimer's disease. I see it in Jim's weekly presence outside the deportation court as he, along with dozens of others, publicly prays for fair and just treatment of undocumented workers. In each of these three examples of the Spirit's patience, people are imitating the self-emptying of Jesus and selflessly responding to God's call for the enrichment of another.

Gentleness is another one of the Spirit's fruits. It is found in people who no longer have the emotional need to pontificate their way through the meeting, bark their demands through the day or pull strings behind the scene to get their way. Ruthless, callous and unforgiving behaviors have ceased and obsession with control and manipulation has dissipated in gentle people.

Sandy exudes gentleness. A single mother of two children, she spent most of her years working two jobs to make ends meet and to provide her children with an education. Often misunderstood and sometimes ignored and ostracized by her family and friends, she very deliberately did what she could, sometimes at great sacrifice, to ensure the very best for her children. This tender, considerate and gentle woman has endured the tribulations of life with the strength of steel. When you ask her where her inner strength and power come from, she raises a finger to the sky and says, "I put everything in God's hands and simply say, 'Let it be done to me according to Your will.'"

Sandy allows the Spirit to guide her in the way of gentleness because she has learned an important lesson: control and manipulation will not always get you where you want to go. When the ego is in the driver's seat, we live driven lives. All of our emotional energy dissipates as we become the pawns of every whim and wish of the ego. In effect, we become slaves to ourselves. Our lives become bloated with gluttony, green with envy and depleted with recreational sex. Anger seethes just beneath the surface, greed stuffs our pockets lest we not have enough, and vanity keeps a mirror constantly before our eyes. Ego-driven lives often spin out of control. Lives that are open and surrendered to the need of this sacred moment, however, become full of gentleness, and free from the need for control.

Self-control, like gentleness, also betrays a life in the Spirit. Rather than being driven and weighed down by the ego's emotional over-investment in hedonistic desires and fleeting passions, we find the Spirit lifting us up to a mountain of self-mastery. This trait is not about extraordinary self-restraint due to white-knuckled willpower, however. It is, instead, about interior freedom.

I see this expression of the Spirit's fruit in a spiritual directee who rarely, if ever, talks about "battling temptations" or engaging in "spiritual combat." By his own admission, he still experiences temptations. However, he speaks of "surrendering his will to God" a number of years ago. Rather than struggling to overcome the ego's initial reaction to a tempting thought or seductive situation, this directee has learned through his continual practice of ongoing discernment how to empty himself for the sake of others. He is free from his ego and can respond to this sacred moment with self-control, based upon the inspiration and guidance of the Spirit.

The selflessness engendered by life in the Spirit brings joy, peace, patience, gentleness and interior freedom. But life in the Spirit doesn't stop there. A person living by the Spirit also has an openness to others which is characterized by the other four traits of the Spirit's fruit.

REFLECTION QUESTIONS

1. How do you experience life in the Spirit? How do you discern the Spirit's presence in your life?

2. What are the practical consequences and implications of John Vianney's statement "It's nothing. It's *only* the devil!" for your own spiritual formation? How can you be more aware of "the postgame show"?

3. How are you growing in joy, peace, patience, gentleness and self-control? What obstacles does your ego put up to block these traits of the Spirit's fruit in your life?

14

THE TRAITS OF OPENNESS

*P*eople led by the Spirit are committed to the everyday duties resulting from past decisions. They also have openness to the unmet needs of others in the present moment. And their commitment and openness are characterized by four more traits of the Spirit's fruit mentioned by St. Paul in Galatians 5: love, kindness, generosity and faithfulness.

STILL MORE SPIRIT-FRUIT
The Spirit of Jesus guides people in the way of *love*. Love is the motivating force behind openness to the required duty or unmet need of this sacred moment. It is also the legacy of Jesus: "I give you a new commandment, that you love one another. Just as I have loved you, you also should love one another. By this everyone will know that you are my disciples, if you have love for one another" (John 13:34-35). It is because of this trait that friendships begin, affection for others develops, marriage proposals are accepted and children are born.

But there is also a challenge inherent in this trait: "But I say to you that listen, Love your enemies, do good to those who hate you, bless those who curse you, pray for those who abuse you" (Luke 6:27-28). In many respects, love of enemy is the acid test of whether or not someone is living in the Spirit or is still a slave to the ego.

For more than half my life, I tried and failed to live up to this challenge, thinking it meant developing the same kind of emotional investment in those who betray me and take advantage of me that I have in my closest friends and confidants. However, a conversation with a Chinese atheist led me to a different understanding of this challenge.

Professor Zhang was my colleague at a Chinese university in Beijing. She had been married for twenty-five years and had one daughter. One evening over dinner, we began talking about the different understandings of marriage that are found in Western and Chinese cultures. In the course of the conversation, I asked her, "When did you realize you had fallen in love with your husband and wanted to marry him?" I was surprised by her response: "Albert, we Chinese find you Westerners somewhat odd in this regard. So many of you make the decision to marry based upon the emotion of love. But you have to realize that emotions come and go; they are not trustworthy enough to make major life decisions upon. We Chinese have traditionally looked upon marriage as something that originates in a decision, a commitment. We make the decision to build a life together and to commit to sharing a bank account together and to having a child together. Over the years, a husband and wife negotiate their way through a marriage. It's almost like your Western understanding of a business deal. For we Chinese, marriage is primarily about a commitment and less about the emotion of love."

As I reflected upon that conversation, it dawned on me that love of enemies is somewhat analogous to the traditional Chinese understanding of marriage. It's less about an emotion and more about a commitment or a decision. Love of the enemy is expressed in the determination to live the golden rule. That's Jesus' understanding of it. Immediately after stating the obligation to love the enemy in Luke's gospel, Jesus explains its practical consequences:

> If anyone strikes you on the cheek, offer the other also; and from anyone who takes away your coat do not withhold even your shirt. Give to everyone who begs from you; and if anyone takes away your goods, do not ask for them again. Do to others as you would have them do to you.
>
> If you love those who love you, what credit is that to you? For even sinners love those who love them. If you do good to those who do good to you, what credit is that to you? For even sinners do the same. If you lend to those from whom you hope to receive, what credit is that to you? Even sinners lend to sinners, to receive as much again. But love your enemies, do good, and lend, expecting nothing in return. (Luke 6:29-35)

Guided by the Spirit, we resolve to stop the cycle of violence. We overcome the ego's temptation to retaliate, to balance the scales of justice, or to take advantage of the person or the situation. We are selflessly open to the enemy's or beggar's need in this sacred moment. This is what self-emptying is all about and this is how love of the enemy is expressed.

Kindness, a second trait of openness, makes a person sparkle with self-forgetfulness, compassion and consideration for others. It often lies behind simple acts of charity and hospitality. I know a person who, a number of years ago, during the forty days of preparation for Easter called Lent, decided that he would perform one deliberate and secret act of charity each day.

It almost became a game for him as he tried to creatively come up with ideas. It also became a way to remind himself that holiness begins with selflessness. Once Easter arrived, he decided to continue with this little daily practice. People who know him today spontaneously use words like *kind, warm-hearted, helpful, generous* and *caring* to describe him. This man is clearly sowing seed in the new life of the Spirit.

Closely connected to kindness is *generosity*. This fruit of the Spirit makes a warm-hearted person a big-hearted person. So much more than secular philanthropy, this trait is born of the conviction that God can be trusted to provide for all of our needs, so we hesitate to hoard. The letter to the Hebrews states,

> Keep your lives free from the love of money, and be content with what you have; for [God] has said, "I will never leave you or forsake you." So we can say with confidence,
>
> "The Lord is my helper;
>   I will not be afraid.
>   What can anyone do to me?" (Hebrews 13:5-6)

And so a person animated by the Spirit lavishly shares personal time, talents and treasures. The ego's obsession with self-preservation has gone up in smoke.

Jesus made a comment about this trait one day in the temple as he watched people put money into the treasury. While rich people were putting in large sums of money, a poor widow came forward and put in two small copper coins worth about a penny. Jesus noted, "Truly I tell you, this poor widow has put in more than all of them; for all of them have contributed out of their abundance, but she out of her poverty has put in all she had to live on" (Luke 21:3-4).

When we live according to the Spirit, we are sometimes prompted to dig deep into our pockets and give not simply from our surplus wealth but from our daily need. This is the heart of Christian generosity and is what distinguishes it from philanthropy.

The Christian communities of Macedonia were a shining example of this trait. In an effort to raise funds for the church of Jerusalem, Paul told the Christians of Corinth,

> We want you to know, brothers and sisters, about the grace of God that has been granted to the churches of Macedonia; for during a severe ordeal of affliction, their abundant joy and their extreme poverty have overflowed in a wealth of generosity on their part. For, as I can testify, they voluntarily gave according to their means, and even beyond their means, begging us earnestly for the privilege of sharing in this ministry to the saints—and this, not merely as we expected; they gave themselves first to the Lord and, by the will of God, to us. (2 Corinthians 8:1-5)

Paul continued by developing what you could call a "spirituality of generous giving," of giving according to your means and even beyond your means. It is based upon "the generous act of our Lord Jesus Christ, that though he was rich, yet for your sakes he became poor, so that by his poverty you might become rich" (v. 9). Indeed, selfless openness to the need of this present moment is done for the enrichment of others in imitation of Jesus. This results in what Paul calls "a fair balance" (vv. 13-14).

The Spirit also guides us in the way of *faithfulness*. This trait is about being loyal and dedicated to public commitments and their resulting consequences. Characterized by unswerving trustworthiness and reliability, it keeps friendships and marriages together, gives hope and security to elderly persons who rely upon others for their care, and gets teachers and professors in the classroom to help educate our children.

Faithfulness is also about being "full of faith." As the writer of Hebrews puts it, "faith is the assurance of things hoped for, the conviction of things not seen" (Hebrews 11:1). The eleventh chapter of the letter to the Hebrews traces this dimension of faithfulness through salvation history, starting with creation, Abel, Noah and Abraham and continuing with Moses, the Israelites, Rahab and others. And then, at the beginning of chapter 12, Jesus is presented as "the pioneer and perfecter of our faith, who for the sake of the joy that was set before him endured the cross, disregarding its shame, and has taken his seat at the right hand of the throne of God" (v. 2). This letter clearly interprets faith as a verb that is centered upon God and not our ego; it is steadfast loyalty and trust in God despite the terrible odds and obstacles placed in our path.

Faithfulness, understood as a life overflowing with faith and trust in God, motivates missionaries all over the world to endure hardship, misunderstanding and sometimes persecution for the spread of the gospel. This fruit of the Spirit inspired my mother, widowed at age forty due to my father's suicide, not to lose hope in the face of getting a professional education and raising three of her five children still at home. Faithfulness galvanized and animated people like Dr. Martin Luther King Jr., Archbishop Desmond Tutu and Nelson Mandela in their battles for civil rights. And, with this trait, the Spirit overcomes all forms of fear and anxiety that the ego uses to paralyze us from taking action.

THE SOURCE OF OUR HOLINESS

When it comes to spiritual formation and the spiritual life, it is impossible to be self-made individuals. Though willpower and self-discipline can sometimes silence the demands of the ego, the attraction and allurement of the ego's obsessions with self-concern, self-image, self-gratification and self-preservation remain. That's why those who have mastered willpower and self-discipline still occasionally feel dispirited, disappointed and discouraged.

The Spirit and the Spirit alone is the source of our holiness. It is only by making the concerted effort to live in, according to and guided by the Spirit, displaying the various traits of life in the Spirit, that we are set free from slavery to self-concern, self-image, self-gratification and self-preservation. The Spirit is the risen Christ's gift to us. As temples of the Spirit, the Spirit already abides within us. Our challenge is to live the "enSpirited" reality of who we are, in other words, with the Spirit as our "operating system."

REFLECTION QUESTIONS

1. Who do you consider to be an enemy? How can you overcome your ego and grow in a commitment to the enemy?

2. How are kindness and generosity expressed in your daily life? Which is more difficult for you and why?

3. How do you experience the transforming power of the Spirit in your own life and spiritual formation? What does it mean to live in, according to and guided by the Spirit?

CONCLUSION

*I*t's late at night. Cindy is watching cable TV and sees an ad for a Christian organization that works with poor children in Haiti. Touched by the ad, she feels called to somehow respond but knows that her husband and children are not in a position to uproot and move to Haiti. Her family is, however, in a position to support a child. She plans to talk to her husband about that in the morning. She's open to God's call in this sacred moment.

Matt is a sales representative for a local radio station. He spends time every day searching for new clients who will advertise on the station. His job affords him flexibility with how he manages his forty-hour workweek. This week he has five great leads that could translate into five new clients as well as a sizable commission for him. This week is also the week that his second-grade daughter appears in her school's afternoon concert. Though Matt is a model employee who faithfully gives eight hours of his day to the station, he is also well aware that this is his daughter's first public performance. It's important to his daughter that he be present. Selflessly open to the duty of this sacred moment, he gets into his car and heads to his daughter's grammar school.

After more than thirty-five years of teaching in college, Phil and Arlene are enjoying their retirement. They have fulfilled their dreams of seeing the pyramids in Egypt and the Eiffel Tower in Paris. In the process of planning a three-month trip to England and Ireland, they found out from a friend's casual remark that a local school was in desperate need of after-school tutors for math and English. After prayer and conversation with others, they temporarily put the trip to the British Isles on hold and decide to respond to the need of their local neighborhood school.

I believe that holiness is not as elusive or impossible as most of us think. That's not to say it's easy; it certainly is not. But I think there are many people in the world like Cindy, Matt, Phil and Arlene who know that God calls them right where they are. Living in and guided by the Spirit, they imitate Jesus: they selflessly respond to God's call in the duty or need of this sacred moment for the enrichment of others.

APPENDIX

- Holiness is a selfless openness and response to God's call in the duty or need of this sacred moment for the enrichment of another. It is done in imitation of Jesus and is guided by the Spirit.

- God's call in the required duty or unmet need of this present moment is an expression of God's will for me. Consequently, *every* moment is sacred.

- Though forms of self-reflection are important in spiritual formation, especially for beginners, there comes a point when I have to move beyond self-reflection and begin to focus on others and their needs. This is the meaning of self-emptying and is the practical expression of love.

- God sometimes speaks in experiences that have an expressed other-worldliness and divine obviousness to them. However, such dramatic experiences are the rare exception. To be attentive only to the dramatic is to potentially miss other ways that God issues a call or reveals a required duty or unmet need in this sacred moment.

- God's call can also be wrapped in something barely perceptible to the human senses.

- God's word is spoken *in* and *through* human experience. Human experience is the megaphone through which God issues a call and manifests the divine will.

- God is truly present in the required duty or unmet need of this sacred moment.

- All creation exists for Christ's glory. Alienated creation comes back into harmony with God and is reconciled through Christ's self-emptying on the cross—his selfless openness and response to the present moment. This is God's will for the world.

- Every time I freely choose to imitate Christ by forgetting myself and enriching the life of another, I help promote the full realization of the kingdom and the lordship of Christ.

- A Christian without a sense of mission is a stunted Christian.

- The three principles of ongoing discernment are (1) the duties and responsibilities of my present state in life are the basic building blocks for the kingdom of God, (2) holiness is oriented toward a healthy lifestyle, and (3) commitment to a church community is required.

- The three practices of ongoing discernment are (1) daily, consistent prayer, (2) spiritual direction, and (3) loving acceptance and trustful surrender to whatever happens at each moment.

- *Lectio divina* and imaginative prayer are helpful in sensitizing me to the call of God and in answering the questions of ongoing discernment, What would Jesus do and how would he do it?

- The examen invites me to revisit the past hours of the day and, sensitive to the thoughts and feelings I experienced, ask where, how and why God was calling in the required duty or unmet need of a particular moment.

- The ego's obsession with self-concern, self-image, self-gratification and self-preservation is the primary obstacle and hindrance to selfless openness to God's call in this sacred moment.

- Jesus teaches that the path to holiness is paved with self-emptying for the sake of others.

- The Holy Spirit plays a central and decisive role in my spiritual formation and the spiritual life. The Spirit not only frees me *from* the ego's obsession with self-concern, self-image, self-gratification and self-preservation but also frees me *for* the enrichment of others.

- I am encouraged to live in the Spirit, according to the Spirit and guided by the Spirit (see Romans 8:5; Galatians 5:16, 25). Such a lifestyle is characterized by "the fruit of the Spirit": "love, joy, peace, patience, kindness, generosity, faithfulness, gentleness, and self-control" (Galatians 5:22-23).

- The Spirit and the Spirit alone is the source of my holiness.

ACKNOWLEDGMENTS

As I finish writing this book, I feel blessed in many ways.

Many years ago, a wise spiritual director introduced me to Jean-Pierre de Caussade's *Abandonment to Divine Providence*. Now, every December, as a way to prepare for Christmas, I take my dog-eared and underlined copy of it off the shelf and reread it. Readers who are familiar with this classic work of Christian spirituality will certainly see its influence upon my current understanding of holiness. *Abandonment to Divine Providence* continually challenges me to look nowhere else but right in front of me for the call of God. What a blessing this book has been.

The names and details of the people you have met in these pages have been significantly changed to protect their identities. I'm blessed to know the real people behind my examples who continue to inspire me to selflessly respond to this sacred moment. They remind me that Christianity is *the* family affair par excellence.

This is my third book with InterVarsity Press. And as the saying goes, "it's been a charm." The employees are always so gracious and courteous when I show up in front of Audrey's reception desk and proceed to disrupt her life and the lives of other IVP employees. Cindy Bunch, my editor, continues to be not only a trusted professional guide and mentor but also a marvelous friend. God blessed me in a special way with my first introduction to IVP four years ago.

Almost thirty years ago, God continued his love affair with me by sending Fr. Daniel Reed of Cleveland, Ohio, into my life. Dan is my closest friend. He never ceases to inspire me as I watch him respond to the duty or need of the present moment. Even in times of personal tragedy and tribulation, Dan shows a selfless love for Jesus. As I dedicate this book to Dan, I also say a prayer of gratitude to God for blessing me with such a holy spiritual companion.

If this book challenges you to take another look at the sacred moment in which you find yourself and momentarily forget yourself as you respond to God's call, then God has certainly blessed me again.

For more information about Albert Haase, O.F.M.,
and his ministry of the Word,
visit his website at www.AlbertOFM.org.